Develop[ing Your]
Leadership
in the Early Years

Also available from Continuum

Observing Children and Young People 4th Edition – Carole Sharman, Wendy Cross, and Diana Vennis
Good Practice in the Early Years, Janet Kay
Working Together for Children, Gary Walker
Learning Through Play, Jacqueline Duncan and Madelaine Lockwood

Developing Your Leadership in the Early Years

Mary Briggs and Ian Briggs

Continuum International Publishing Group
The Tower Building
11 York Road
London, SE1 7NX

80 Maiden Lane
Suite 704
New York, NY 10038

www.continuumbooks.com

British Library Cataloguing-in-Publication Data
A catalogue record for this book is available from the British Library.

ISBN: 9781847062338 (paperback)

Library of Congress Cataloging-in-Publication Data
Briggs, Mary (Mary J.)
Developing your leadership in the early years / Mary Briggs and Ian Briggs.
p. cm.
Includes bibliographical references.
ISBN: 978-1-84706-233-8
1. Early childhood education–Administration. 2. Children–Services for–Management. 3. Educational leadership. I. Briggs, Ian. II. Title.
LB2822.6.B75 2009
372.12–dc22

2008047245

Typeset by Newgen Imaging Systems Pvt Ltd, Chennai, India
Printed and bound in Great Britain by Athenaeum Press Ltd., Gateshead, Tyne & Wear

Contents

Introduction

Chapter Outline

Introduction

This book is intended for anyone working within children's services, which include the provision of day care or nursery facilities. The settings you are likely to be working in may be children's centres, schools, nurseries and community projects. This book will also be of use to people from different professional backgrounds and is not aimed at educational professionals alone. We hope that this book will support you if you are

- studying early childhood studies degrees or other social science degrees leading to working in children's services;
- studying to become a teacher in the early years;
- already working in the children's service and 'emerging' as a leader;
- an experienced leader preparing for or studying National Professional Qualification for Integrated Centre Leaders (NPQICL);
- or reviewing your leadership after previous study and development.

Throughout the book a focus will be on the different standards for professionals working. in the early years. The rest of this introduction will look at these standards and their similarities and differences. These can be found in the Appendix on Professional Standards, on page 113. Turn to these now and look at the range of the Standards expected depending upon professional background.

As can be seen the expectations are different according to the role and professional background in each of these sets of standards, and this reflects the diversity of settings in the early years and the range of employers for whom staff may be working. There are though similarities in the expectation to take on more leadership responsibilities with more senior posts.

Reflective task

Look carefully at the standards applicable to your role or the role to which you aspire. Are you confident that you can locate yourself clearly within these standards? Jot down some of the key features of those standards. Now look at the other professional standards. What are the key similarities and differences? Are there standards that all have in common? What is the focus of these differences?

Further chapters

Each of the chapters in this book will be linked to the appropriate standards for all of these professional backgrounds working in the early years. You will find the details of all of the standards referred to in each chapter in the Appendix. This will enable to you select aspects that will be most useful to you when developing your leadership and work on those for yourself. There will also be a summary of key ideas at the end of each chapter that we hope will be helpful to you as you use this book. Each chapter will also have research summaries, which will give you an overview of leadership research from different professional perspectives, and these are referenced so you will be able to follow up the original text if you are interested in a particular starting point. The other features of each of the chapters are the reflective tasks, which invite you to explore specific ideas introduced and link these to your current professional working context or the context for which you are training. Finally there are a number of checklists or inventories with which you can begin to explore your own understanding and your own development needs. You may read this book from beginning to end, but you may be more likely to dip in and out of specific chapters as and when the issues become relevant to your leadership development.

Summary of key ideas in this chapter

- There are a number of different leadership standards that apply to the early years depending upon your professional background.
- The standards have some common features but there are significant differences.
- You will have become more familiar with the standards within the early years.
- You will have an overview of this book and how you might begin to use the material here for your own development.

Further reading

CWDC (2007). Guidance to the Standards for the award of early years professional status. Leeds: CWDC

DfES/DWP (2003). National standards for under 8s day care and childminding http://www.surestart.gov.uk/_doc/P0000411.PDF Nottingham: DfES (accessed 21.09.08)

DfES (2004b). National Standards for Headteachers. Nottingham: DfES

DfES (2007). National Standards for Leaders of Children's Centres. Nottingham: DfES Publications

McDonnell, F. and Zutshi, H. (2006). (HZ Management and Training Consultancy) *Mapping of leadership and management standards for social care*. Leeds: Skills for Care http://www.topssengland.net/files/prod3%202edn%2006webedn(1)(1).pdf (accessed 21.09.08)

Useful websites about professional standards

http://www.cipd.co.uk/about/profstands

http://www.cwdcouncil.org.uk/

http://www.ncsl.org.uk/

http://www.tda.gov.uk/teachers/professionalstandards.aspx

http://www.teachernet.gov.uk/_doc/11525/Professional%20Standards%20for%20Teachers.pdf

All the above websites were last accessed on 21.09.08.

1 What is Your Current Leadership Experience?

Chaper Outline

Unless you have a title that includes leader you probably may not see yourself as a leader or having had any significant experience of leadership. If this is true for you it is also true of a large part of the population, despite many ordinary individuals having huge innate leadership capacity. This chapter will assist you in exploring those ideas and how your experiences to date have and will influence your leadership as it develops regardless of your current position in the workplace. You will also be thinking about the experiences you have and how you can begin to develop those skills and knowledge further, but throughout the book we will argue that leadership development is a journey – perhaps without a destination! The other concept that you will explore is how being led has influenced your ideas about leadership.

Standards that this chapter will help you explore are:

Early Years: S34
Social Care: Functional area A, Functional area D
Children's centre leaders: 1. Leading learning and development (1.8), 3. Being accountable and responsible (3.6)
Teaching: Q32, C40, E13, A2, A3, Developing self and working with others

By the end of this chapter you will:

- have explored your own experiences of leadership
- have audited your leadership experiences
- have explored how being led has influenced the development of your ideas about leadership

Leadership without being an obvious leader or having a leader's title

All out experiences influence our lives in some form or another. This is to most a very obvious statement. Yet if you are already working with children in a setting you will know that how others treat them influences their learning about relationships and how to make new ones. We tend to feel more comfortable thinking about this in relationship to children than in relation to our own learning. If you think about your school life as an example of part of the learning process you are likely to have had favourite subjects, favourite teachers and groups of friends and the things you did together either in or out of school. You may also have had less than positive experiences of subjects at secondary school, teachers you may have found it difficult to get on with or contemporaries who at the time appeared to delight in making your life a misery. Together these experiences have coloured your attitude to education. Were you an only child? Did you have leadership roles in your family or among friends? Were you a member of a club like guides or scouts where you had a clear leadership role? What children's literature inspired you? All of these have had an influence on your existing orientation towards leadership and the skills and knowledge you possess. It may be that in preparation for your work in early years you gained some experiences like teaching dance classes, swimming instructing or similar where you led the activities that both children and adults participated in. Again these activities develop leadership skills in relation to many things such as planning and preparing and possibly even negotiating what actually took place. If you asked your friends about you, are you seen as the one with the ideas about what your social group should do? A ringleader? Think about how you influence others in the groups in which you operate. It is interesting to note that much of the leadership research that you may come across doesn't look explicitly at the role socialization plays in leadership experiences and this perhaps is particularly ironic as a major focus of early years settings is the effective, ethical socialization of young children, helping to provide that essential platform to become socially integrated adults.

Reflective task

Try to complete the following grid.

⇨

Name/ function of the group to which I belong	What is my relationship with the other members of this group?	What if any is my specific role in this group?	How long have I been a member of this group?	Did I have a choice about being a member of this group?	Has my position in the group changed over time?

What is interesting to reflect upon is the static nature of some group membership for example your position in the family may not change but over time the relationships may alter. If you have just started work somewhere you may feel that you are seen as a 'junior' member of staff, but this is likely to change as you gain more experience in your current role and how this might develop over time. This is why we are now changing our thinking about leadership.

Auditing your leadership experiences

In the following grids for you to complete you are encouraged to consider your experiences to date and therefore your starting skills base for leadership.

Personal experiences

Activities	A lot of experience	Some experience	No experience
As a child I was the person in any group who decided what we were going to do			
I was a scout/guide leader			
I took on responsibility for younger siblings or other peoples children			
I led a sports team			

Activities	A lot of experience	Some experience	No experience
I coached a sports team			
I put myself forward for representative tasks e.g. student rep for committees			
Other people put me forward for representative tasks e.g. student rep for committees			
I scribe for group tasks at work or during studies			
I report back for group tasks at work or during studies			
I volunteer to take on projects on my own			
I volunteer to take on projects with others			

Experiences

Experiences	Lots of different experiences in different situations	A reasonable amount of experiences in a narrow range of situations	Limited or no experiences
Being in charge of groups of children			
Being in charge of groups of adults			
Being responsible for induction of new staff			
Being responsible for organizing events/activities			
Working in groups with others either at college on course, in the work place or other			
Being responsible for bookkeeping/accounts			
Leading the planning for an organization			
Planning activities for groups of adults			
Supervising the work of other adults			
Giving feedback to adults about the their work performance			
Writing policies and procedures			
Reviewing policies and procedures			
Talking to parents and carers about their children			
Discussing children and families with other professionals			

(Continued)

Experiences	Lots of different experiences in different situations	A reasonable amount of experiences in a narrow range of situations	Limited or no experiences
Working alongside other professionals to run groups/activities or events			
Dealing with conflict between adults			
Dealing with complaints made to the organization			
Celebrating successes			

Skills and knowledge

Skills/knowledge	Very confident	Confident	Not at all confident
Organizing work rotas/timetables of events			
Contributing or writing SEF documents			
Writing action plans			
Budgets and financial planning			
Chairing meetings			
Writing minutes			
Delivering reports to committees			
Consultation meetings with parents/carers			
Working with other agencies			
Booking meetings/events			
Selling/cold calling/leafleting/door knocking			
Time management and prioritizing work			
Taking part in the recruitment and selection of new staff			
Taking part in the induction of new staff			
Taking in part in supervision session for staff			
Setting targets for staff performance			
Giving feedback on staff performance in their role			
Gaining feedback from others about your own performance as a leader			
Leading staff development sessions			
Taking part in Common Assessment Framework (CAF) meetings in relation to safeguarding children			

Skills/knowledge	Very confident	Confident	Not at all confident
Demonstrating practice of skills/knowledge			
Dealing with conflict or complaints			
Celebrating the success of others			
Celebrating your own success			

You will see that you have already got a range of experience upon which to build even if you feel that the amount is quite limited at this stage. If you are just starting with your career this is not surprising but this will quickly change as you focus your continued development. You may have plenty of experience of some things, for others more limited experience and maybe no experience for other areas. This might be as a result of your focus say in a nursery within a school or children's centre as an example so you have lots of experiences of safeguarding and contact with parents but more limited experience of working with other adults outside the nursery. If as we assume you want to broaden your experiences and develop your skills then you will be able to see clearly where your attention might be focused.

Keep your notes from this activity to use as a basis for planning your leadership development later in this chapter and in following chapters.

Being led by others?

Throughout our life those who have led or lead us influence our leadership experiences. This may start with our relationship with the brother or sister or friend who led us in trouble or who had wonderful ideas for games and activities within the family or friendship groups. We may also have had jobs where you have strong opinions of those who have led us. We may have seen 'managers' as inflexible partly because they don't appear to have listened to our requests for time off at a particular time or those who may have appeared to have no authority and little respect from others working with them.

Reflective task

Consider the leaders who you think have led you well.

Try to identify what it is that they did or do that made this relationship feel successful for you working with them. Sometimes thinking about specific incidents that have occurred can help you clearly identify behaviours in the leaders.

Specific incidents	What the leader did	What did they say	Specific order of actions	Specific other behaviours that you have identified	Outcomes

Can you see any trends in the kinds of behaviours that you feel were most successful for you being led? Do you think this would be the same for others led by the same person or would they perceive things differently? If you can, try sharing the outcomes on your completed grid with someone who also knows the same leader to gain a more objective view of the behaviours you have identified. Do you each see the leader in the same way? This raises the issue of how we see people and the fact that we react to people and their behaviours differently depending upon our own experiences and relationship with the leader in this case. So when we look at what has worked for us with different leaders we need to be aware that the same kinds of behaviours may gain different reactions for those we might work with in future.

Now try to do the same for the less positive experiences you have had being led by others. Can you identify specific trends in the behaviours from both situations positive and less than positive? What part did your relationship with/or attitude to a leader have on your perspective? This is important as sometimes we can find it hard to see the other person's perspective until we are in the same situation, and we can appreciate the complexities and/or the wider view of the organization or specific issues that arise. An example of this might be how a parent views a child being out at night and the anxiety that may cause the parent. The child knowing that they are safe perhaps doesn't bother to contact anyone and doesn't see the issues that a worried parent might raise when they return home. On becoming a parent you suddenly realize the depth of anxiety not knowing can cause an individual. Another example would perhaps involve being in a position to see the 'bigger picture' in relation to something that someone has raised in the workplace, and the individual is only seeing the specific case and not the implications for everyone else.

Specific incidents	What the leader did	What did they say	Specific order of actions	Specific other behaviours that you have identified	Outcomes

Specific incidents	What the leader did	What did they say	Specific order of actions	Specific other behaviours that you have identified	Outcomes

From all the tasks in this chapter jot down a few notes for yourself about the kind of leader you want to be or to become. Can you identify behaviours that you would wish to emulate in the role of leader? Are some of the things that you have identified linked to the leaders personality? Is yours the same kind of personality? Would you be able to work in the same ways? If you can, try sharing the outcomes on your second completed grid with someone who also knows the same leader to gain a more objective view of the behaviours you have identified. You may find it useful as you read this book to come back to these ideas at specific times and reflect how your ideas have changed after reading, carrying out activities or gaining further experience.

Starting your action plan for leadership

No one starts without any experience; we all bring different kinds of experiences to a work place. It may be that you are used to organizing your brothers and sisters in a large family or that you have had work experience in a shop and not much with children. In both these examples you will have developed strategies for organizing and dealing with potential conflicts or disagreements. You may not always see your own experiences as directly relevant, but you will have learnt from them even if what not to do next time! Some of you may have much more experience of a range of settings and so can look more closely at the kinds of experiences you have had and plan for your career in Chapter 9. At this stage you may only be starting to plan your leadership development around the kinds of experiences you might want to gain. Try to think of different ways you might gain this like shadowing people in their roles, reading, watching videos or programmes like teachers.tv, visiting different settings or other ideas rather than thinking about courses to attend. Courses do have their place, but they should not be seen as the only development opportunities that you can benefit from. There is more in this book about developing your role and your career in Chapters 7 and 9.

Reflective task

From the information gained in the earlier tasks in this chapter try to complete the following grid. Don't identify more than six things you wish to gain more experiences of at this stage and include things that you already know you can do to develop them further as this is not intended to be a deficit model for development. You may also find it helpful to link the areas of development to the standards appropriate for the role you are aiming to take on in the future.

Specific areas identified	How might you gain more experience of this area	What is needed in order that you can gain the experiences needed	Who might you need to work with to gain the experiences	What do you think you would gain from this experience	Timescale

Summary of key ideas in this chapter

- It is important to realize that everyone has had experiences of leadership in different situations.
- No one starts from a zero position in relation to their experiences, skills and knowledge.
- All our previous experiences influence the development of ideas, skills and knowledge of leadership.
- Our experiences of how others have lead us influence the development of our personal leadership styles.
- From initial knowledge about our experiences, skills and knowledge of leadership we can plan how we want to develop as leaders.

2 What is Leadership?

Chapter Outline

[There are] almost as many definitions of leadership as there are persons who have attempted to define the concept.

Stogdill (1974:259)

In this chapter we will explore how leadership is defined. Wherever you are in relation to your leadership skills we will take you through some of the key theories in an historical overview of leadership development, which will include theoretical perspective from outside early years and as well as within this field of study. At the outset we would like to emphasize that the study of leadership is a highly dynamic issue, and has as we have seen made some significant leaps in the understanding and appreciation of leadership theory in the last decade or so. We would pose the question – is the funding and research into leadership being influenced by external social, political and economic drivers more important than understanding leadership in professional contexts? So much of the leadership research is situated in current social and political thinking. This is why some researchers dismiss historical leadership and attempt to supersede thinking, but the research from the last 100 years has been situated in the social mores of the time. As a further cautionary note it is always wise to bear in mind who funded the research; it was, and is not unknown for researchers to deliver exactly what the sponsors were looking for! The research explored in this chapter will be drawn initially from a wide range of fields of study and different professional perspectives, which we think will be helpful to your own exploration of leadership in the early years.

Standards that this chapter will help you explore are:

Early Years: S34
Social Care: Functional area A, Functional area B, Functional area C, Functional area D
Children's centre leaders: 1. Leading learning and development, 3. Being accountable and responsible, 4. Shaping the present and creating the future
Teaching: Q32, C40, E13, E14, A2, A3, Shaping the future, Leading learning and teaching, developing self and working with others, Managing the organization

By the end of this chapter you will:

- have explored where the notions of leadership have come from;
- have explored how critical notions of leadership have changed over time;
- have explored how general theories and perspectives of leadership can be used to explore the early years context

Leadership and position

Leadership is a word people associated with a position of authority and power to make decisions and direct others to complete tasks. Leaders are assumed to have a certain status with organizations based on their position and title. The truth of the matter is that when you strip leadership back to its component parts it can be achieved without power or authority. It is then we can see it as being about having some form of positive influence over others. If you think about the leaders you know and maybe admire, the names that come to mind are often the charismatic individuals. People like Nelson Mandela who appear to have something extra special about their personality and their influence are often cited when others are asked about leaders. In contrast if you consider the people who have influenced you they are likely to be parents, siblings, friends, teachers and colleagues. The influence may be based on their position of 'power' over you but often it is not a direct control. Were you the leader of a 'gang' of friends at school, the oldest child in the family? The experiences we have early in our lives are part of our 'baggage' carried throughout our lives that has a direct impact on how we learn and develop as leaders.

Reflective task

Pause for a moment and think about your experiences to date. Jot down your position in the family and how this has affected your ideas about leadership. Who have been the influential figures in your life so far? Who are they and what was your relationship with them?

Where do ideas about leadership actually come from?

We have already said that we tend to look at key public figures as the immediately recognizable leaders. Other areas that we might think of that are linked to their position and status are those like the armed forces, politicians or figures in history. In the early research into leadership this led to the 'great man' or 'trait theory', best exemplified by the large numbers of biographies written about great business, political and military leadership. It is assumed in this theoretical stance that these great leaders have something that other people don't have and that if this is not something you already possess you can't learn how to do this, in many ways it is seen as an innate trait. The reason for this was that research focused on existing successful leaders, and white males dominated this group. This group of people had self-confidence in their ability to lead as they had been in many cases brought up expected to take on leadership roles in society. As a consequence the research resulted in theories about leaders based upon this group of people. Pearn and Kandola (1993) have shown that 80 per cent of senior managers talk about a male when they are first asked to describe a successful manager. The same is true if the question is phrased in relation to leadership. This focus on males who are already successful leaders didn't represent all the possible forms of leadership and leaders there might be. Although this early work focused on leadership much of the material written in this period is actually looking at management with success measured by measurable outcomes such as overall organizational performance as expressed through profitability and other tangible measures. This underlines how dominant the commercial and military sponsors were in driving forwards the thinking on leadership. It also started to ask the question how transferable many of these dominant notions were. Was for instance, it suitable to apply notions of leadership drawn from a commercial setting to schools and politics? So much of the 'great man' theories of leadership are also situated in the dominant thinking and concerns of the time, the fact that many commercial organizations – the most powerful and dominant at the time were oligopolies, many having lost their sons in the fields of Flanders of World War I were looking for sound and predicable ways to search out those suitable to take the reins of what were family dominated businesses. The fact that research into leadership in other settings was not taking place is not an indication that leadership was seen to be an appropriate concept, it was more that there was no source of funding for research into these settings.

During the middle of the twentieth century the pace of leadership research quickened markedly. Again we have to be wary of where the research was sourced, who was funding it and what outcomes were being sought as with the benefit of hindsight we can see how drastically this affected the outcomes of research.

Another key milestone was the advent of psychologists publishing and finding audiences for the early thinking into personality. Many blind alleys were explored here with some researchers and commentators arguing for 'extroverts' making the best leaders. They argued for extroversion being synonymous with great oratory and exceptional communication skills. Others who championed the idea of introverts making the best leaders pointed to the brooding silence and reflective nature of such archetypes as pointed to high levels of intellect and precision in thinking and accorded these attributes to effective leaders. The competition between these schools of thinking was ultimately proved to be futile; individuals invested with great leadership capacity were found to exist in both populations. Recently there has been more work undertaken on notions of leadership preferences defined by personality type, but again much of this lies in the realms of unproven and unsubstantiated research.

The next advance in leadership thinking came about as a response to the school of scientific management as championed by F. Winslow-Taylor (Taylorism) (1911) and McGregor (1960) and Theory X *v* Theory Y. This led to popular bipolar models of leadership. Those who had a preference for autocracy were superior leaders to those who had a preference for involving others, 'participative' leaders?

Again this led to researchers and commentators falling into two competitive camps. Some could point to autocratic leaders driving organizations to ever increasing levels of profitability while others argued for participative leaders shaping their organizations to having happier more fulfilled employees. It is worth remembering that the 'Hawthorn' experiments had clearly shown that happy engaged employees when interest was shown in them they performed at higher measurable levels than those who were not engaged by their leaders. It would be dangerous even today to dismiss many of these thoughts, we are now beginning to see from studies by those such as Mike West et al. (2001–2008) in the Aston papers that organizations where there are higher levels of concern for the attitudinal health of employees, as measured through general achievement motivation and the presence of such things as acceptable social support in the workplace are the organizations that have demonstrably higher levels of performance than those that disengage their workforces.

A further significant step was taken with the emergent thinking in the 1960s around task definition being the determinant of leadership approach. Researchers such as Blake and Mouton (1985) and Feidler (1964) were influenced by military thinking in the post-World War II period where experiments were designed to pinpoint leaders in more or less random groups of soldiers. These approaches were to become defined as 'emergent leadership in leadership groups'. As most of these approaches were conducted in times of war and conflict by government, foremost among which were the US and British (WASBe – War Office Selection Boards) they became subject to restrictions for security reasons and it was a half a century before reputable researchers obtained the outcomes to evaluate. The basis of these experiments were composed of exercises where if you presented groups with often ill-defined tasks or tasks with complex and challenging solutions who were the people who were likely to emerge as leaders? The thinking was if leadership emerged in these controlled circumstances then it was safe to assume that they would perform as effective leaders in critical conflict situations. The fact that many of these emergent leaders proved to be highly inept leaders in warfare brought these approaches into severe disrepute, but they had the advantage of encouraging researchers to ask questions around was it the nature of the task being performed, and demanded whether that was the determinant of the leadership approach required or was it the orientation and sensitivity that individuals had towards others. This debate was to roll onwards for decades and it can still be felt today.

In recent years it has become fashionable for many to dispel these 'situational' approaches to leadership. In fact we feel they still have an awful lot to offer managers and professionals who are developing as leaders. Where Blake and Mouton (1985) asked the question, what leadership approach was required when two independent scales of concern for task as opposed to concern for people interplayed it gave us the now infamous managerial grid. This was further exposed to much public acclaim in the 1960s by Blanchard who introduced the idea of a four-box approach in his work on situational leadership. This has given rise to many versions of questionnaires for use in leadership and managerial development, some with higher levels of face validity than others. Again Blanchard took a significant step; he introduced the idea that the needs of the follower were a key determinant in the approach a leader had to take. The idea of follower 'maturity' was for many a significant step forward in contemporary leadership thinking. Here, the follower's 'maturity' increased with exposure to tasks and situated work environments as determined by the leader. With low maturity the leader's role is to 'tell' the follower, instructional approaches are appropriate but rapidly move with increasing maturity of the follower to 'selling'. Once the 'immature' follower has understood and begun to grasp the basics of what is demanded of them in their role they may challenge and ask 'why'? When this occurs, then simple telling will become ineffective and the need to the follower will change, the tactics of the leader are then to give reasons as to why things are done in the particular way demanded and then as the maturity continues to develop the leader has then to involve and invite the follower to participate in the task, and then as the follower achieves maximum maturity the leader can increase social distance from the follower and delegate to them and leave them to progress at their own pace.

Even some 30 years or so ago there was concern among academics that the world of leadership research was becoming confused and polarized. Ralf Stogdill undertook a review of the leadership literature and in 1974 published a thorough evaluation of the theoretical basis for understanding leadership; his conclusion was that there was no real conclusion to be drawn although there were the first signs that a new approach was needed. The demands of employers were changing; there was a need to scientifically understand what makes individual leaders effective and by the 1980s a new revolution began, again generated in

North America and new schisms opened up between those who were advocating an approach to leadership that was based upon individual charismatic notions and those who were advocating visionary leaders.

How people become leaders

Bass' (1989, 1990) theory of transformational leadership suggests that there are three basic ways to explain how people become leaders. The first two explain the leadership development for a small number of people. These theories are:

- Some personality traits may lead people naturally into leadership roles. This is the Trait Theory.
- A crisis or important event may cause a person to rise to the occasion, which brings out extraordinary leadership qualities in an ordinary person. This is the Great Events Theory.
- People can choose to become leaders. People can learn leadership skills. This is the Transformational Leadership Theory.

Leadership types

The charismatic leader: these are the leaders who gain prominence by strength of personality.

The traditional leader: these are the leaders whose position is assured by birth – kings, queens and chiefs or landed gentry, first sons or children of the firm's founder.

The situational leader: these leaders develop through effectively being at the right place at the right time.

The appointed leader: these leaders assume the power arises directly out of the position they hold.

The functional leader: these leaders influence arises from what they do or as a result of expertise in a specific area.

The principle-centred leader: these leaders power is evidenced with regard to equity justice and integrity.

Trait theory

This section begins to unpack the different aspects of trait theory in relation to leadership where most of the research work focused on existing leaders and tried to unpack what were the key behaviours that they shared to make them the leaders they had become. This research was not really interested in previous experiences and in many cases they were judged to be successful because they had reached the position of leader in large corporate organizations and did not acknowledge the support of those working with and for them. Bennis and Nanus (1985) in their book *Leaders*, published in 1985, they describe leaders as people who

- keep their attention focused all the time on what they are trying to achieve – their goals;
- use their communication skills to influence their teams so that they share the same goals;
- clearly, consistently and reliably communicate what they mean and stick to it;

- have a strong sense of their own worth and skills, and keep trying to improve themselves and their performance.

What you gain a sense of is that these leaders are very focused individuals with a clear sense of purpose for their role as a leader. Traits are linked to the individual's personality regardless of their position within an organization.

John Kotter (1996) in his book *Leading Change* described how people with the skills needed to be effective leaders show this, by using their personal power rather than their positional power.

Positional power is the power that comes from the [job] position you hold: 'I am the team leader; you must do what I say.'

Positional power means that you reward people for doing what you want, and punish those who do not.

Personal power means that others believe in you and trust you to make the right decisions. This is because your behaviour has shown that you deserve this trust, making you the obvious choice to decide what to do.

Still the focus is on the individual alone in a leadership position, and as a result of this kind of research employers were looking for leaders who had specific characteristics something extra that most people didn't or don't have with a key example of this being charismatic behaviour traits.

Charismatic and great leaders

One trait that links to the focus on existing leaders is charisma. These people are those at the centre of attention, appearing to have outgoing personalities, able to engage others with inspirational rhetoric and behaviour. These people are sometimes seen as 'hero innovators' having the energy and drive to take an organization forward. We associate the same characteristics with world leaders in the media or history. These people come into the category of leaders born to the role rather than people who have developed the skills to become leaders.

Considerable attention is given in the research to notions of great leaders as being the role models for everyone else in leadership positions or aspiring to leadership roles. This can be rather off-putting when you begin to unpack the expectations. Kouzes and Posner (1987) identified what they saw as the ideals of great leadership.

- Challenge the process – first, find a process that you believe needs to be improved the most.
- Inspire a shared vision – next, share your vision in words that can be understood by your followers.
- Enable others to act – give them the tools and methods to solve the problem.
- Model the way – when the process gets tough, get your hands dirty. A boss tells others what to do . . . a leader shows that it can be done.
- Encourage the heart – share the glory with your followers' heart, while keeping the pains within your own.

These ideals appear hard to live up to. Can mere mortals even achieve the same levels of greatness? Are these reasonable expectations?

The last model for leadership in this section also focuses on behaviours but they are around four frameworks.

In the Four Framework Approach, Bolman and Deal (1991) suggest that leaders display leadership behaviours in one of four types of frameworks: Structural, Human Resource, Political or Symbolic. The leadership style can either be effective or ineffective, depending upon the chosen behaviour in certain situations.

1. The Structural Framework

   The 'structural' leader tries to design and implement a process or structure appropriate to the problem and the circumstances. This includes

   - clarifying organizational goals
   - managing the external environment
   - developing a clear structure appropriate to task, and environment
   - clarifying lines of authority
   - focusing on task, facts, logic, not personality and emotions

   This approach is useful when goals and information are clear, when cause–effect relations are well understood, when technologies are strong and there is little conflict. When there is low ambiguity, low uncertainty and a stable legitimate authority.

2. The Human Resource Framework

   The human resource leader views people as the heart of any organization and attempts to be responsive to needs and goals to gain commitment and loyalty. The emphasis is on support and empowerment. The HR leader listens well and communicates personal warmth and openness. This leader empowers people through participation and attempts to gain the resources people need to do a job well. HR leaders confront when appropriate but try to do so in a supportive climate.

   This approach is appropriate when employee morale is high or increasing or when employee morale is low or declining. In this approach resources should be relatively abundant; there should be relatively low conflict and low diversity.

3. The Political Framework

   The political leader understands the political reality of organizations and can deal with it. He or she understands how important interest groups are, each with a separate agenda. This leader understands conflict and limited resources. This leader recognizes major constituencies and develops ties to their leadership. Conflict is managed as this leader builds power bases and uses power carefully. The leader creates arenas for negotiating differences and coming up with reasonable compromises. This leader also works at articulating what different groups have in common and helps to identify external 'enemies' for groups to fight together.

   This approach is appropriate where resources are scarce or declining, where there is goal and value conflict and where diversity is high.

4. The Symbolic Framework

   This leader views vision and inspiration as critical; people need something to believe in. People will give loyalty to an organization that has a unique identity and makes them feel that what they do is really important. Symbolism is important as is ceremony and ritual to communicate a sense of organizational mission. These leaders tend to be very visible and energetic and manage by walking around. Often these leaders rely heavily on organizational traditions and values as a base for building a common vision and culture that provides cohesiveness and meaning.

This approach seems to work best when goals and information are unclear and ambiguous, where cause–effect relations are poorly understood and where there is high cultural diversity.

Reflective task

When you read about any theoretical model to describe situations it is important that you spend some time thinking about the ideas. Pause for a while here and consider the ideas that have been introduced to you here. Which appeared to make the most sense to you? Did any appear to resonate with your current practice or the observable practice of a leader you are working with? Which models did you find difficult to understand or didn't appear to apply to any practical context?

If you can, try and discuss your thoughts about these ideas with others as the process of discussion can be helpful to clarify your own ideas. It is important to note that the models presented here are a selection of a wide range of potential models of leadership, and it is not expected that you will agree with them all.

Getting into leadership

'I am not a leader of men since I prefer to follow,'

From the Nickelback song 'Leader of Men' (2000)

Although this is taken from a rock song this phrase echoes the sentiments of many people in their working context. They have a preference to follow and let someone else do the leading. So what happens when people become leaders? How do they get into leadership positions? In discussing this with NPQICL (National Professional Qualification for Integrated Centre Leaders) participants many felt that they had not made a conscious decision to become leaders, and they had almost become the leaders by chance. For some it was about stepping up to take on the role when a leader moved on from the organization or for other reasons wasn't there to continue in the leader's role. On other occasions it was the influence of others suggesting that they apply for a post to take on the role of leader, and without that external influence they would not have considered even applying. It is however interesting to note that with our experiences of working on leadership development programmes in a variety of sectors we have found that when exploring personal leadership stories many have described the process of assuming leadership positions as awakening from a dream to find oneself in the reality of some difficult positions that they were accountable for sorting out.

Research (Rosener 1995) suggests that women in particular do not even consider applying for posts unless they are confident that they can do the majority of tasks required in the job specification. This can become a real barrier to women's progress in organizations even in areas where the workforce as a whole is predominately female. (More about leadership and careers is dealt with in Chapter 9.)

Having applied for or taken on the role of leader people can feel that it is only a matter of time before they are found out, they haven't got the skills and knowledge expected of a leader.

The dangers of feeling like a fake

Kets de Vries (2005) explores in his article the fact that in many walks of life including business there are leaders who believe that they are complete fakes. To the outside observer, these individuals appear to be remarkably accomplished; often, they are extremely successful leaders with staggering lists of achievements. These 'neurotic impostors' as psychologists call them are not guilty of false humility. The sense of being a fraud is the other side of being capable and causes a great many talented, hardworking and competent leaders to believe that they don't deserve their success. They think they have 'Bluffed' their way through life and they are haunted by the constant fear of exposure. With every success, they think, 'I was lucky this time, fooling everyone, but will my luck hold? When will people discover that I'm not up to the job?' In his career as a management professor, consultant, leadership coach and psychoanalyst, Kets de Vries has found neurotic impostors at all levels of organizations. In this article, he explores the subject of neurotic imposture and outlines its classic symptoms: fear of failure, fear of success, perfectionism, procrastination, and workaholism. He then describes how perfectionist overachievers can damage their careers, their colleagues' morale and by allowing anxiety to trigger their self-handicapping behaviour cripple the organizations in which they work. Finally, Kets de Vries offers advice on how to limit the incidence of neurotic imposture and mitigate its damage through discreet vigilance, appropriate intervention and constructive support.

Harvey and Katz (1985) identified the phenomena of how so many people in leadership positions were seemingly incapable of internalizing their own strengths and attributes, even when they were easily recognized by others. They were instrumental in coining the phrase 'imposter syndrome' – this has been associated with a great deal of thinking and research around the efficacy of women leaders in the workplace but not exclusively women but also individuals differentiated by age, disability or ethnicity.

Reflective task

Current leaders

Think about your current position and how you arrived in your leadership post. How do you think you got here? Was this a planned progression or have you arrived almost by accident? Try to be honest

⇨

about how you feel your skills and knowledge match the role you have. Does the 'feeling like a fake' apply to you? Do you at times feel like an imposter in your role? If you do feel like a fake when does this occur and what circumstances might bring this about?

Aspiring leaders

Think about your current position and the leadership elements within your current role. Is this an area that you would like to develop or have you uncertainties at the moment about seeing yourself in the role of leader?

Situated leadership

Leadership can be seen, as more than a few traits or preferable behaviours. Failure of leaders to gain consistent results led to researchers examining situational factors as one of the biggest influences on leadership and its effectiveness. The situation appeared to determine the appropriateness of leadership style; the task of the leader is to see which styles are the most appropriate in each situation.

Fiedler (1964) named his model 'the Leadership contingency model' and it is based on the theory that the leader adopts an appropriate style based on the favourableness of the situation. The three factors that contribute to favourableness are

- the leader's relationship with others
- the degree of structure of the task
- the leader's power and the authority of their position

Principled leadership

Covey's (1992) model of leadership is based on the idea that effectiveness in a social role such as management depends on how far a manager abides by a certain set of principles. The degree to which managers keep to the principles of trustworthiness, trust, Empowerment and alignment decides their fate, either success or oblivion.

Covey introduces a moral element into management and identifies eight characteristics of principle-centred leaders. Within this approach leaders are seen to have the following characteristics:

- Continuous learning
- Service oriented
- Radiate positivity
- Believe in people
- Lead balanced lives
- See life as an adventure

- Synergistic (a catalyst)
- Exercise for self-renewal (balance emotionally as well as spiritually, physically and mentally)

What implications do these theoretical perspectives have for leaders working in the early years field?

One big issue when looking at the existing research on leadership is the fact that it started by looking at existing leaders who were successful and they tended to be 'white western and male'. Many of the characteristics identified among those who were successful potentially meant exhibiting 'male' characteristics in order to seen as successful leaders in the same way. A review of the early childhood leadership literature by Muijs et al. (2004) identified a very limited specific research in this area. Of the existing work Rodd (1996, 1997, 1999, 2006) as an example focuses more on management despite the titles of publications including leadership and the practical aspects of roles in the early years. Most case studies involve self-reporting of the skills and knowledge the leaders feel they need.

'In addition to being kind, patient, warm, nurturant and so on, effective leaders were perceived . . . to be goal-oriented, having a planning orientation, assertive, proactive, professionally confident, visionary, influential and a mentor or guide' (Rodd 1996: 122).

It is interesting to see that the female leaders in this New Zealand study are looking for traits as in the early work on male leaders in other contexts.

Participants in Scrivens' (undated) research based upon Rodd's work identified the following characteristics of leadership as important for them:

- being a consultative leader
- sharing power
- being a good communicator
- a supporter of teachers and a promoter of good teaching
- commitment to children
- commitment to the ethos of the service
- having a vision for the service

As we can see this is very educationally focused and although collected as self-reports in the specific contexts has a quite narrow view of early years provision and the professionals who work in this area. It is also interesting to note from everything explored earlier in this chapter about the initial starting point of leaders who were seen as successful by others that this research starts with exactly the same group of leaders.

Some see the context as so specific that they dismiss the existing leadership research as not relevant and are therefore in danger of losing much valuable work that can apply to early years even if not generated in that context. This book seeks to draw upon a selection of existing research that can be helpful for leaders in the early years. Little of the work with the exception of Aubrey (2007) makes links with theoretical perspectives from others' leadership and management research outside the field of early years. The gender of most leaders in early years is touched upon by Rodd (1999) who suggests that women have difficulty in identifying leadership. This may be as many of the early years organizations have very flat structures rather a hierarchy and the nature of the work results in everyone collaborating towards the provision of the service. The impact of leadership on the performance of others as well as the impact on quality is picked up in this book in Chapter 6 as part of the challenges for leaders.

Ebbeck and Waniganayake (2003) in their book *Early Childhood Professionals: Leading Today and Tomorrow* focus on three areas, administration, management and leadership with the emphasis on the management side of the roles. They do pick up strongly on the gender issue in relation to leadership in the early years describing the early childhood profession as a 'pink ghetto'. They argue that traditional models of leadership haven't worked in the early years because of the way people work in these settings; however, this is based upon a specific view of early years services which is itself changing in different countries with the development of integrated approaches to services for children and their families in which only part of the function is early years 'educare'.

This chapter has only provided a brief overview of some of the developments of ideas about leadership generally and then begun to relate them specifically to early years. Hopefully this has given you some starting points for further reading about leadership.

Reflective task

What are the key issues that you have identified from this chapter? Which resonate with issues from practice? What have you found to be the least useful? Try to identify why areas either resonate or don't appear to apply. Try also to discuss these issues with others as that process can help to clarify your own thinking.

Are there areas that you would like to follow up? Jot down either the issues and/or the names of researchers to read more about.

Summary of key ideas in this chapter

- Leadership is a complex area of study and activity in the workplace.
- Notions of leadership have come from initially exploring the characteristics of successful male leaders.
- Much of the research has focused on behaviour traits of the leaders.

- The focus on traits meant a view of leadership as something you either have the necessary traits to be able to do or not – it could not be learnt.
- The other ways of looking at leadership are those which start from principles or the situation.
- When we get to be a leader we may 'feel a fake' about gaining that position and that this is not an uncommon feeling.
- Research in early years is relatively new and still developing and has not really established itself in relation to other existing research on leadership in different contexts.

Further reading

Bass, B. (1990). From transactional to transformational leadership: learning to share the vision. *Organizational Dynamics*, Vol. 18, Issue 3, Winter, 1990, 19–31

Bass, B. and Avolio, B. (1993). Transformational leadership and organizational culture. *Public Administration Quarterly*, 17, 112–121.

Ebbeck, M. and Waniganayake, M. (2003). *Early Childhood Professionals. Leading Today and Tomorrow*. Eastgardens, NSW: MacLennan and Petty Pty Ltd.

Pearn, M. and Kandola, P. (1993). *Job Analysis: A Manager's Guide*, 2nd ed.

London: Institute of Personnel Management

Stogdill, R. (1974). *Handbook of Leadership: A Survey of Theory and Research*. New York: Simon & Schuster Adult Publishing Group

Leadership and Management 3

Chapter Outline

The terms leadership and management are often used interchangeably in the literature and in the ways people describe their roles in the workplace. This chapter seeks to explore the similarities and differences between the terms and the relationship between them in roles in the early years. The role and knowledge of leadership versus attitudinal are dealt with in Chapters 3 and 4.

Standards that this chapter will help you explore are:

Early Years: S34, S35, S36

Social Care: Functional area A, Functional area B, Functional area C, Functional area D, Functional area E and Functional area F

Children's centre leaders: 1. Leading learning and development, 3. Being accountable and responsible, 4. Shaping the present and creating the future, 5. Managing the organization

Teaching: Q32, C40, E13, E14, A2, A3, Shaping the future, Leading learning and teaching, developing self and working with others, Managing the organization

By the end of this chapter you will:

- have explored the differences and similarities between leadership and management
- considered the key ideas about the two terms and their relationship
- developed your own ideas about the relationship between the two terms and what this means for your current role

What is the relationship between leadership and management?

What is the relationship between leadership and management? Can they operate independently? In leadership roles there are tasks to be undertaken but there are also the less tangible notions of the vision for the setting, organization and ideas about the direction it will take. While these are not the concern of just one person the leader of any organization is expected to have a clear picture of where it is going and how it might get there these are more long-term strategic aims rather than short-term operational goals.

Shift from management to leadership

One of the key identifiable trends of recent years has been the shift from management towards leadership. The issue of leadership is one that either excites and engages audiences or bores and terrifies in equal measure. For many, leadership is an issue that still carries with it baggage that is associated with elitism, sexism, unbridled power and models of historic 'heroes'. However, here we argue that the implicit notion of leadership has changed. The approach we take here is as far from the 'hero – innovator' as we can get. We need to explode the myths that surround leadership and begin to see that it is a force for change and a force for good. So what are the myths?

The first myth that is still perpetuated is that leadership is a very rare commodity, invested in only a tiny proportion of the population. This is clearly nonsense. We would not have brought about such root and branch change in our society if we did not have a plethora of leaders. Leadership is all around us, the problem may be that we do not recognize it and use the wrong lenses in the microscope when we want to look at it closely.

The second myth is that there is a requirement for leadership at the top of the organizational tree; it is the most senior people that are leaders, they have to make the very difficult decisions and have to engage with staff at all levels to bring about change and transformation in organizations (Chapter 8 develops these ideas further). The fact remains that there is an acute shortage of leaders at the top of organizations and if anything this is becoming worse. When we have looked at what criteria is used to select, promote and recruit managers there is little about leadership in there. In many organizations the choice of who takes the reins is one based on a mixture of managerial, professional or social connectability criteria.

The third and perhaps the most dangerous myth is that leadership is difficult. To be an effective leader you need near superhuman powers to influence others, yet we are slowly beginning to learn that effective leaders do extraordinarily ordinary things to be effective.

It is for these reasons we feel that leadership has been an issue that has misled us for too long. Maybe we have taken policy makers too much at face value in recent years too. Many of our public services have been berated and criticized for lacking leadership and while this has been demotivating at times we need to rethink why this has come about.

A phenomenon that has not had enough debate is what has happened in the move to decentralize and promote subsidiarity. Over the past ten years the picture of service provision has changed out of all recognition with greater localization. Schools – for good or ill – have greater levels of local control, government at all levels is localizing decision making at the lowest possible level and the concept of choice is still being promoted as an easy way to engage members of the public and service users. All this has put the spotlight on people who run and provide services at a local level. These people have to manage and lead, they have complex decisions to make and little freedom and flexibility at the same time. They are regulated at a National level and audited at a local level, performance managed to extraordinary levels of detail and at the same time have to be customer focused, change orientated and still be able to take their staff with them.

Manager or leader?

A manager is concerned with orderly structures, day-to-day activities, getting work done, monitoring outcomes and efficiency.

A leader is concerned with interpersonal behaviour, a focus on the future, change and development.

A person can be a leader, manager, both or neither.

Leadership

'Leadership is that process in which one person sets the purpose or direction for one or more other persons and gets them to move along together with him or her and with each other in that direction with competence and full commitment' Jaques and Clement (1994: 4).

Management

'Management is efficiency in climbing the ladder of success; leadership determines whether the ladder is leaning against the right wall' Covey (1992: 47).

Managers and leaders – a comparison

Managers	Leaders
are analytical, structured, controlled, deliberate and orderly	are experimental, visionary, flexible, unfettered and creative
use the power of the logical mind	use the power of intuition
concentrate on Strategy	nurture culture
follow rules and procedures	pursue visions
isolate	correlate
determine the scope of problems	search for alternative solutions
seek markets	serve people
think about rivals and competition	think partners and cooperation
correct strategic weaknesses	build on strategic strengths
wield authority	apply influence
instruct	inspire
manage by goals or objectives	manage by interactions
control	empower
react	are proactive
reorganize	redevelop
scrutinize performance	search for potential

Source: Adapted from Hickman (1990)

This table adapted from Hickman's (1990) book *Mind of a Manager, Soul of a Leader* is not an exhaustive list of the differences but we hope that it will help you to identify some of the differences and similarities between the roles.

Reflective task

Existing leaders

If you are already a leader, consider which category you would place yourself in having read the traits associated with managers and leaders? Are there differences depending upon what you are doing during the day?

Aspiring leaders

Think of a leader you know or work for and where you would place them in relation to these traits. Can you discuss this with someone else who knows the same leader to compare perceptions? Or even the leader themselves to gain their view of their role?

People or task orientated?

The Blake and Mouton *Managerial Grid* (1985) uses two axes:

1. 'Concern for people' is plotted using the vertical axis.
2. 'Concern for task' is along the horizontal axis.

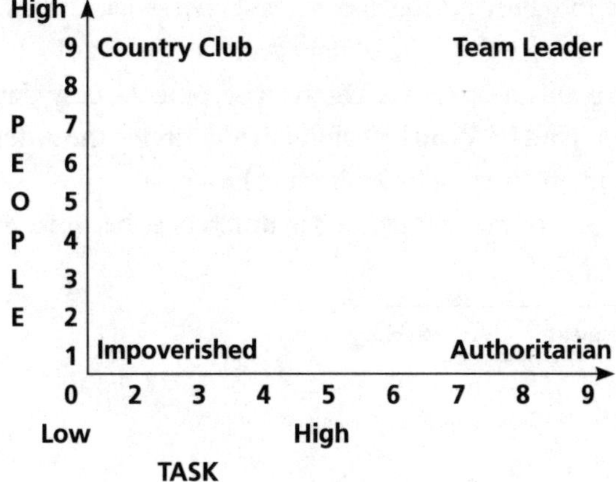

Most people fall somewhere near the middle of the two axes and by going to the extremes, that is, people who score on the far end of the scales, Blake and Mouton come up with four types of leaders:

- **Authoritarian** (9 on task, 1 on people)
- **Team Leader** (9 on task, 9 on people)
- **Country Club** (1 on task, 9 on people)
- **Impoverished** (1 on task, 1 on people).

Reflective task

You may find it useful to consider where you would place yourself on this grid. Does your position stay the same when the activity changes? Though the titles of the types of leaders may not feel appropriate to the context, what is important is the switch and a leader's awareness of how they operate in different situations at work.

Metaphorical differences

Many metaphors are so commonly used, including both '*market*' and '*customer*' that they have become '*dead metaphors*' whose metaphorical roots have been forgotten. The pervasiveness of metaphors and their ability to translate the complex and unfamiliar into something familiar and simple to grasp, mean that philosophers, linguists and social scientists are increasingly agreed that they are fundamental to structuring our view of the world and how we behave within it (Lakoff and Johnson 1999). Whether we use them consciously, or without thinking, metaphors can be shown to play powerful roles in how we create and perceive business organizations and their behaviours (Grant and Oswick 1996; Morgan 1986).

Metaphors are often used to describe and illustrate the differences between leadership and management and this can lead to a polarizing effect where management is seen as bad or at least inflexible and leadership is seen as good and creative. They can become the only way we are able to see the concepts. On the other hand they can be helpful in identifying the different strands of management and leadership in our current or aspirational roles.

The following grid gives a few examples of metaphors for the differences between management and leadership.

Management	Leadership
Execute	Direct
Male	Female
Hard	Soft

Leadership without management

This can mean setting a direction or vision that others follow, without considering too much how the new direction is going to be achieved. Other people then have to work hard in the trail that is left behind, picking up the pieces and making it work. Example: In the early years this might be seen as setting a direction for the provision for children by bringing in a different approach such as forest schools but without considering how this change might be implemented in a specific setting and what would be needed to support the changes to practice.

Management without leadership

This can mean controlling the resources to maintain the status quo or ensure things happen according to already-established plans. Example: In the early years this might mean sticking to rules and not being able to work with events that occur during the day without prior planning. This can feel very restricting for practice and its development.

Leadership combined with management

In this situation leadership and management work together and set a new direction and manage the resources to achieve it. Example: This acknowledges that specific changes to practice do require a clear sense of direction which is agreed and plans for supporting any changes to practice, thinking through the practicalities involved and making sure that support is available.

Some potential confusion over the relationship between leadership and management

These can occur when one element either the leadership or the management appears to be absent. The absence of leadership/management is not to be confused with participatory or facilitative management, which can be a very effective form of leadership.

Also, the absence of leadership should not be confused with the type of leadership that calls for 'no action' to be taken.

It would seem that we have arrived at a point where we think we can have great managers who are perhaps not so great leaders, but it would be hard to find highly effective leaders who are ineffective managers. This has though come under challenge in recent times when we can point to individuals who are socially prominent leaders but are not called upon to manage in normal or the occupational sense of the word. Great thought leaders who can mobilize public opinion are used as examples. Popular influential characters who lead and champion causes – without mentioning names we are referring to those who front awareness and fund-raising festivals, and without besmirching their managerial reputations it would be hard to identify their talent as managers in occupational or organizational settings, but they are unquestionable thought leaders. Imagine though for one moment what it would be like if you had a highly inspirational thought leader as a boss who was less than able to manage the day-to-day needs of the organization without becoming bored? It is perhaps this that emphasizes the need for management as much as the need for leadership. We might live in an age where leadership is the focus of attention, but it is vital that we have competent and able managers as well. But, we have to leave the question open as to whether investing in less than effective managers is a sound strategy to follow if we need to increase the supply of leaders.

It is valuable to reflect on early research work that was undertaken to ensure a supply of effective talent in organizations which indeed did see effective management as the pinnacle of effectiveness. Management was about logic and rationality and leadership was getting very little treatment at the time.

An example to draw on in the argument for management is the great lengths that the public service is currently going to in adopting project management techniques. An approach to project management that is near universal is PRINCE 2. This is a project management methodology that is incidentally owned by the UK government. It grew out of large-scale information technology implementation that was highly complex with huge numbers of interdependencies within projects. When faced with such complexity it is abundantly clear that a systematic, logical, clear and transparent process is needed to ensure that such projects are delivered on time. It is highly probable that many newly established early years centres were in fact established with such project management methodology being applied. It is when we look at large-scale complex projects that we can see that although it is fashionable to talk leadership, a world without management could be a very dangerous place to be. It is not that effective leadership does not play its part in the formation of logical approaches to complex systems, it is more that effective leaders take a different approach and are attenuated to different aspects of problem resolution.

Reflective task

Can you think of a situation where you were faced with a complex issue to resolve? Think through how you saw this through and can you draw up two lists, one containing your leadership response and the other containing your managerial response to the issue in hand?

Don't worry if you found this a very hard – perhaps even impossible – task to try and do. What it does suggest is that we as individuals find it hard at times to be able to separate out the differences in what we do. To paraphrase, a participant on a leadership development programme that one of the authors worked with some time ago when a plenary debate raged on the differences between management and leadership: 'Ah – I see – leadership is about doing management but in a leadership way and not in a management way.'

Management, leadership and change in organizations

When we apply our thinking about the differences and distinctiveness of leadership and management we can see through a particular research study around the leadership of change where these differences lie. From Jerry Hunt, a US researcher, we can see not just the differences between leadership and management, but how they interplay to ensure that we manage changing circumstances through the application of both leadership and management.

Hunt (1991) studied a number of emergent and expanding businesses; he applied the organizational life cycle in the following way,

Stage in organizational life cycle	Managerial and leadership application
Birth – when a new organization is formed – this can be applied to the establishment of a new enterprise or the creation of new spin-out organizations in the public service domain.	Organizations in this stage of the life cycle require high levels of leadership. Hunt was particularly applying notions of Transformational leadership here from Bass (1990). The rationale was that high levels of inspiration and motivational influence are needed here. Leaders are persuasive and have the ability to paint a clear and unambiguous picture of what this organization (or setting) is going to be like. They are highly effective at winning support and gathering and marshalling the enthusiasm of others vital in energizing the infant organization onto the next stage.
Growth – here the organization (or setting) is becoming established and growing both physically and metaphorically. Its reputation is becoming established and the patterns are becoming predictable and systems and procedures are needed to put boundaries of control around what happens in the organization or setting.	While there is still a requirement for leadership that provides energy and motivational inspiration and to ensure that talented people stay with you the control mechanisms demand that managerial talent is required. At the growth stage it may be that managerial functions are more visible in the day-to-day operations the organization contains. Meetings become more formalized and rules, processes and procedures are refined to ensure growth is maintained and that staff keep a focus on the systems needs of the organization.

Stage in organizational life cycle	Managerial and leadership application
Maturity – while the organization may continue to grow and expand and its reputation becomes more established – the organization is learning that it has grown as a result of the systems, processes and procedures that it has put in place to ensure its survival.	At the heart of Hunt's work is this notion that established organizations fall into a pattern of behaving. Organizational paradigms have been established and there is a corporate memory to draw upon. Organizational cultures and established practice and may be hard to change. Management as opposed to leadership has ensured the growth and fought off any competitors – the belief is established that the systems and procedures that the organization has have become the reasons for its survival; it sees management as the means of sustaining itself. Staff motivation and morale are seen to be products of the efficiency of the system and not as a product of the leadership capabilities of those in managerial positions. The ***critical issue*** is that any organization cannot survive on this alone. When it is faced with critical challenges it will try and manage its way out of trouble. It may indeed become blind to the motivational needs of its staff even though it may restate its mission statement in a way that says its staff are its biggest asset. Here Hunt noted that it was the organizations that tried to manage their way out of inevitable trouble that sank into organizational oblivion but those that chose to re-energize leadership went into another more aggressive growth cycle.
Death!	The organization or setting that relied on managing out of trouble.
Rebirth	The organization that leads its way out of trouble – the organization or setting that applies the inherent curiosity about how people see the task were those who went on not just to survive but to prosper.

Source: Adapted from Hunt (1991)

Reflective task

Think through either your current organization or one that you have been familiar with in the past. Think through any stage in the above model and try to characterize the balance between the leadership and managerial approaches that were taken at the time. Did you ever experience working in an organization in its maturity that tried to manage its way out of trouble?

Transactional and transformational leadership

Bass, although he has been one of the researchers and academics who has held prominence in the field of leadership research for almost a quarter of a century would still be regarded as a 'new paradigm' leadership researcher. Although the origins of 'transformational' and 'transactional' leadership came from political as opposed to occupational notions of leadership (James McGregor – Burns (1978)) Bass (1990) is still seen as the internationally recognized figure in the field in what has become to be known as transformational leadership. He does however place a great deal of emphasis on the need for management. A key concept introduced by Bass was the intersection of two independent variables that of the effectiveness and ineffectiveness scale. This was overlaid with the active and passive scale. Bass reasoned that an individual has choice and discretion in the roles they occupy in how they convey their desires and wishes into instructional behaviour to staff. A close examination of the model clearly places transformational leadership at the pinnacle of effectiveness and being 'active'. This he argued is a discretionary approach – a leader (or manager) can choose to display behaviours that are effective if they are made aware of what those behaviours are. This he stated was the realm of leadership. But he also places his notion of effective management by choice in the effective and active quadrant, but by definition it sits at the lower effectiveness scale than leadership. If an individual were to stay at this level they could be accused of sub-optimizing their performance – the developed transformational leader needs to be critically aware of what is demanded of them to become a fully functioning transformational leader.

By implication the less self-aware manager can apply choice and discretion to occupational scenarios – interestingly Bass chose to go back to managerial practice notions from the 1950s in applying the concept of management by exception, management by exception being how an individual manager chooses to become involved and requires staff to only engage them when it is required. This may be when a particular interpretation of an instruction of clarification of how any particular rule or command is to be operationalized. It was drawn from early thoughts on managerial efficacy when a manager's time may be used on only those matters where he or she is required to act. Bass does here draw a distinction between management by exception (MBE) active – when this is a reasoned and active choice to put space and distance between themselves and staff for positive results and management by exception passive. We need to see management by exception passive as being different from total abrogation, the 'laissez faire' idea of the psychologically as well as perhaps physically absent leader or manager. Management by exception passive is again a conscious choice but it is passive in nature, distanced from staff and may be gone to at times a selfish end that is concerned with self-aggrandisement at the expense of effectiveness. Even in MBE passive there is a small intersection with the active and effective quadrant in the model. This is perhaps when there are accidental effective outcomes from the lack of presence of the manager or leader.

Reflective task

Can you think of a time when you have experienced this management by exception? One issue for many integrated services for children and their families is the distance that some staff are either from the centre of most activities due to lone working and outreach or the location of activities. As a result these staff do not come into contact with their immediate line manager often during a working week and even more rarely do they have any contact with more senior staff.

> If you are leading and managing staff and their work how often do you see them face to face during the week? What impact does this have on their perception of you as a leader and manager?

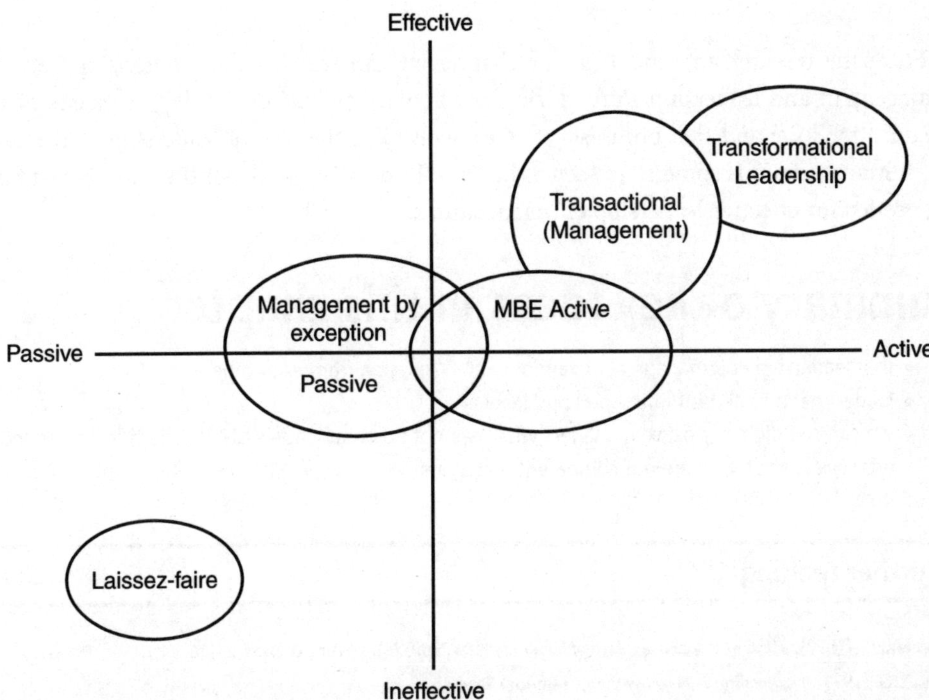

Source: Adapted from the theoretical perspective of Bass and Avolio (1993)

Although this model is a useful way of thinking through the interrelationships between the concepts of management and leadership there are however a few reflective criticisms that we can make. Although Bass has argued for leadership being a highly active notion (in fact some US commentators have said that leadership is a contact sport and not a virtual reality) it might be worth exploring the thought that some leadership activities may be passive by intention. Although Blanchard's leadership cyclical model sees leaders increasing social distance as the maturity of the follower increases (and we can see these models of leadership being more about management than leadership today), Bass's model does not account for the managed and intended increasing of social distance that effective leaders may choose to employ in leaving space for talented staff to fill to encourage them to develop. Others would argue that this is in itself an active choice of the leader.

Reflective task

Consider the strategy of creating distance to allow 'leaderfulness' to develop in others. Does this work? Do people feel abandoned? Are you as a leader explicit about the space you might be creating for others to develop?

From the research presented in this chapter we can see that the relationship between management and leadership shifts during any activity or part of the day or phases of the organization's life and that both aspects are involved in the role of leadership in the early years. Management is sometimes seen as bad and leadership good, but the truth is that both are needed for effective leadership of organizations.

Summary of key ideas in this chapter

- that leadership and management cannot exist in isolation from each other
- leaders need to be both managers and leaders
- we can see highly effective managers who may not be great leaders but it is hard to find rounded effective leaders who are not competent managers

Further reading

Hickman, C. (1990). *Mind of a Manager, Soul of a Leader.* New York: John Wiley & Sons

Hunt, J .G. (1991). *Leadership: A New Synthesis.* London: Sage

Lakoff, G. and Johnson, M. (1999). *Metaphors We Live By* (2nd ed.), Chicago: University of Chicago Press

4 New Paradigms in Leadership

Chapter Outline

When we look back at the recent history of research into leadership we can see that many of the ideas that were in fashion fitted with the current social thinking. Also, we have to be careful about who has historically financed the research into leadership. The fact that many of the ideas about leadership that are in circulation today were sponsored by individual commercial organizations and even the military means that we have to cautious about transferring them from one setting into another. The converse can apply too, because we have new emergent ideas from say the social care sector does not mean that we automatically dismiss them it just means that we have to ask the question about how these ideas apply our specific setting. In this chapter we look at some of the emergent new paradigms of leadership, many of which arise from a variety of disciplines and we ask you to critically think through how they apply to early years settings. Theory also emerges from shifts in the context for specific leadership roles. Early years is an area that has had significant changes made to it over the past five years resulting in some very different kinds of roles for leaders for example the children's centre leader. This has meant that although some of the existing knowledge about leadership can apply to the context some doesn't fit and therefore it is an appropriate time to establish new paradigms. This chapter will take you through some of the theoretical shifts in relation to leadership and hopefully point you in the direction for developing your own thinking about leadership in the early years.

Standards that this chapter will help you explore are:

Early Years: S34
Social Care: Functional area A, Functional area B, Functional area C, Functional area D
Children's centre leaders: 1. Leading learning and development, 2. Stronger families, stronger communities, 3. Being accountable and responsible, 6. Building and strengthening teams
Teaching: Q32, C40, E13, E14, A2, A3, Shaping the future, Leading learning and teaching, developing self and working with others, Managing the organization, Securing accountability, Strengthening community

By the end of this chapter you will:

- have explored different ways of looking at leadership
- considered some techniques that will assist in your understanding of current issues for leadership
- developed your understanding of leadership theories

Leadership – it's a contact sport not a virtual reality

The concept of 'Managerial Self Awareness' MSA

In recent years we have asked the question what has all the recent investment in large-scale leadership development really delivered? In asking this question we are not being in any way critical of the excellent work that many people are doing in specialist and academic intuitions throughout the country but are feeling an element of anxiety over what real difference it is making. Simply knowing more about the theoretical basis for leadership does not a better leader make!

There is however the potential for many myths around leadership to be perpetuated – the fact that leaders have to be 'charismatic' or that they have to have phenomenally powerful abilities of oratory are still myths that are in certain quarters perpetuated. Some of the very best leadership experiences are to be found in the ordinary day-to-day behaviours that we can all display. Offering a sympathetic ear to a staff member with an issue or taking the time to encourage a member of staff to achieve a slighter better outcome from a situation they are dealing with through coaching and supporting them are some of the most significant leadership moments. The trouble is we pass through them without stopping to think that this is leadership in practice. The conclusion is that leadership in practice is about ordinary behaviours and not always about exceptional behaviours or even Einstein levels or insight into complex problems.

For many going back to some simple concepts is a great starting point to think about your leadership. Even highly effective people have to constantly review how their impact is interpreted by others, even for people they know well and have high levels of confidence in. The secret here is to be aware of the feedback we are given by others, we are of the opinion that the most effective leaders go to great lengths to encourage others to give them feedback, they spend time and put a great deal of effort into balancing the day-to-day exchange with others and creating the condition where they can elicit others views on how they are doing. A simple how did you think that went followed by can you think of anything I could have done differently or better is a sign that an individual is aware of their personal impact on others.

As the leadership landscape changes the one area that is remaining constant is the knowledge that the closer any individual rates themselves in any performance assessment to the way that others rate them, especially staff is an effective predictor of their leadership abilities. The critics of this say, and occasionally with justification, that there are times when leaders have to do things that others do not agree with or even like if they as leaders are to change things for the better, but that the research (Atwater and Yammarino 1992) consistently points to this harmonization of self-perception to the perception of others is a critical and key determinant of effectiveness.

An effective starting point for you to think through what this means for you is to go back to a simple yet effective feedback idea, the JOHARI window (Luft and Ingham 1955). As Burns (1786) put it, 'O wad some Power the giftie gie us To see oursels as ithers see us! . . .'

The JOHARI window is a simple four-box model.

	I Know Self	I don't know
You know	The 'Arena'	The blind spots
You don't know	The façade	The unknown – or the box of potential

In this model the top left hand box is where we tend to operate with others – the arena. When two people meet they will tend to talk to each other in terms that helps to establish who they are and maybe a little of what personal values they have. The conversation may go a bit like this:

> . . . Hi, good morning . . . I hope you had a better journey to this meeting than I did. The traffic was horrendous this morning and I did not think I was going to get the kids to school on time.

Reflective task

Take a moment to think about what is in this opening conversation. What is the 'self' telling the other person? Make a list of all the explicit and importantly the implicit information this opening dialogue contains.

The 'self' is in fact saying a lot more in one sentence to the assumed stranger than just a complaint about the traffic. Are they saying they have an element of anxiety they are bringing with them? What are they saying about their personal, family and parenting lives? Quite a bit. They are in fact putting things in the 'arena' that they want the other to know. Making a statement about themselves as a person is critical if you want to get others to understand where you are coming from.

If we develop this conversation a little further let's have a look at another dynamic they may be introducing.

> Person 1. . . . Hi, good morning . . . I hope you had a better journey to this meeting than I did. The traffic was horrendous this morning and I did not think I was going to get the kids to school on time.
>
> Person 2. Yes, I was uncertain of what way to travel this morning too, the traffic doesn't seem to get any better even when the schools are on holiday either.
>
> Person 1. I think it must be just the time of year. I am finding that I have hardly any time to prepare for meetings, I read the agenda through a couple of times and I think there are a few things on it that are going to be very interesting . . .

Reflective task

Take a moment or two to think through this last statement from person 1. Is there anything there that may be designed to hide something?

Although it just a hypothesis, person 1 may be thinking that they are highly unprepared for this meeting, and there are things going on that they have little understanding of and they are feeling defensive, nervous or even exposed by being at the meeting. This may be what is going on the façade box. Making statements that while in essence are not always true they represent a true reflection of how the person is feeling. They may not feel safe in coming out and saying to a stranger that they have done insufficient preparation for the meeting but they are saying that have at least read through the agenda. They are saying something quite neutral in effect but are not making a direct statement of how they are feeling about the meeting.

There is a tendency to see the façade box as being a negative place to be, but in careful analysis of exchanges in dialogue between people, whether they are familiar with each other or whether they are strangers is a telling insight into the way they prefer to interact with others. It is not about lying but about finding an acceptable way of beginning to establish an adult, one to one exchange with another. Extreme examples of exchanges in the façade can be created when we are following the important but usually unwritten rules of how to behave in business and occupational environments. To come about and say "cor I had one of a hell of a night last night, didn't sleep well and I think I had too much red wine" may not be a good or even acceptable way of starting a conversation but acting outside the accordance of the way that we feel either physically or emotionally in complying with important rules of engagement at work. Therefore we can see that the façade can at times be a useful place to be. Even though effective leadership may be about transparency and openness in opinion and behaviour there may be times when we have to act out of accordance with our feeling.

Being in the façade can of course also be a very negative place to be, we can say things or even convince people we are feeling a certain way about an issue or an exchange, but it can be an unethical response to avoid being drawn into a situation that we would much prefer to avoid. The façade is a place where ineffective leaders often hide, making excuses about not talking issues that are important to another or as can be the case saying we are not stressed about something or an issue when clearly we are. Too much time in the façade can be a way of transferring stress to another person.

Let's dig a bit deeper. At the end of this meeting,

> Person 2. to person 1.
>
> I really thought you handled that accountant really well in there. The way you persisted in getting an answer on that audit issue was very impressive.
>
> Person 1. Oh I have always had problems with talking to people who deal with the money side of things . . . they can be difficult and talk in accounts jargon that I try to understand but it just confuses me even more.
>
> Person 2. But from where I was sitting it looked really good, you kept on and on at him and your questions were brilliant. Person 1 Oh I must be more careful in future then, I don't think going on and on with someone is a very good thing to do . . .

Reflective task

Where would you place this exchange in the JOHARI window?

Here person 1 is almost afraid to admit they did a good job. Hearing positive feedback is often harder than hearing good feedback.

Leadership and institutional theory – an emergent issue for early years settings

What rules do organizations follow? Do they follow rules that are clearly articulated, set down by institutional leaders or are people in organizations led more by the implicit rules and processes that can take a while for a newcomer to appreciate or even be aware of?

Researchers in the 1960s when looking at prisons asked whether inmates chose to follow the explicit rules laid down or were they more influenced by the dominant rules that existed within the social system. Unsurprisingly the most powerful rule formation came from the inherent social order created through large numbers of people being forced through circumstance to be together that was dominant. These ideas were developed by many others for example DiMaggio and Powell (1983) linking institutional theory and isomorphism.

In recent years this has led to a large body of research thinking that has deep implications for leaders and is of particular significance to those developing their approach to leadership.

Commentators have noted that organizations can take on a life of their own, whether we are talking about small emergent institutions such as early years centres of large multinational corporations, each has a life of its own that can be described as being independent of the formal leadership of the organization. However, there are two dominant perspectives on this issue. The first is how leaders 'imprint' upon organizations. We have seen how in the past leaders have left a legacy upon the culture, values and even the isomorphic structure of organizations. In those organizations that are characterized by bureaucracy we can often see where a particular leader who has been in a post for a time can leave a behavioural and perhaps cognitive imprint. This is explained by the power of their behaviours being so pervasive that others, less dominant in the hierarchy have acquired the behaviours and values systems through processes of collusion and compliance with powerful leaders and continue to replicate them long after the powerful leader has gone. In the mid-twentieth century Herbert Simon (1991) introduced the notion of 'bounded rationality'. He noted that in many organizations what was seen as rational was only accepted because it accorded with the prevailing values systems that were felt to be conditional to that particular organization. This was of course the imposed values of the leadership community, or individual. Anything that did not accord was not seen to be rational, and therefore it was argued would not be adopted, no matter how rational this notion was deemed to be by those external to the organization.

We think this is one potential explanation as to why new leaders are often in the position of finding it hard to engage with a new setting; until they have become confirmed into the organizational rationality they are unacceptable. They are outside the 'sense making' of the rational boundary of the organization made up of people who share in an inherent rationality that is not overtly articulated. Until the new leader has learned to speak the institutional language they are alien and unacceptable. Conversely the new leader can have enough power potential to alter the inherent rationality of the organization but there may be an extreme price to pay for this. As in real language learning some people find it difficult, and if staff struggle to acquire the new language they will pay a price in higher stress levels, disconnectivity from the organizational process, loose role clarity, motivation and purpose. If the inherent rationality in the organization has more power than the new leader then it may be that they pay the price and they become removed from the organizational setting and seek opportunities elsewhere.

The implications for leaders in early years settings are significant here, largely because we suspect that the relative newness of these settings may not have allowed for established inherent languages to develop and that the rationality boundaries may have not been always clearly established.

Reflective task

When you started a new job think about:

a. What were you told formally about the rules, norms and values of the setting you were entering?
b. Contrast the thoughts you had about (a) above with what you subsequently acquired as critical information about the rules that enables you to function in the setting.

Institutional theory and organizational design – implications for leaders

Ethical and authentic leadership

Ethical leadership can be traced back to the ideas of Plato, but it has more recently become an area of discussion as a result of concerns about how we treated each other and our environment. Considering ethical principles provides the foundations for various modern concepts of work, business and organizations. This broadens individual and organizational priorities far beyond traditional business aims of profit. Ethical factors are also a significant influence on institutions and public sector organizations, for which the traditional priorities of service quality and cost management must now increasingly take account of these same ethical considerations affecting the commercial and corporate world.

The modern concept of ethical organizations encompasses many related issues including:

- organizational social responsibility – or simply social responsibility
- the 'triple bottom line – these are the values and criteria for measuring organizational success'
- ethical management and leadership
- 'Fairtrade'
- globalization (addressing its negative effects)
- sustainability
- social enterprise
- mutual organizations, cooperatives, employee ownership
- micro-finance
- well-being at work and life balance

Emotional leadership or leading with emotional intelligence

Goleman et al. (2004) describe six styles of leading that have different effects on the emotions of any followers. It is important to appreciate that these are styles and not types; as a leader you can use any style and the situation or the Reflective task or the followers will determine the most effective style to use at a particular time.

- The Visionary Leader
- The Coaching Leader
- The Affiliative Leader
- The Democratic Leader
- The Pace Setting Leader
- The Commanding Leader

Community leadership

A focus on Community leadership arose from looking closely at the role that democracy plays in working with communities. Part One of the Local Government Act 2000 enshrines in law the role of community leadership, giving councils the new power to promote the well-being of their area. The Audit Commission breaks down community leadership into three separate areas:

- Local democratic leadership is about bringing people together to develop a vision for the area and deliver services to improving the lives of local people.
- Leadership through Partnership is about delivery of services through partnerships between public, private and voluntary organizations. Local Strategic Partnerships (LSPs) are part of this to bring all the partners together.
- Communities leading themselves is about developing the social capital in others to become engaged and take on leadership within the community.

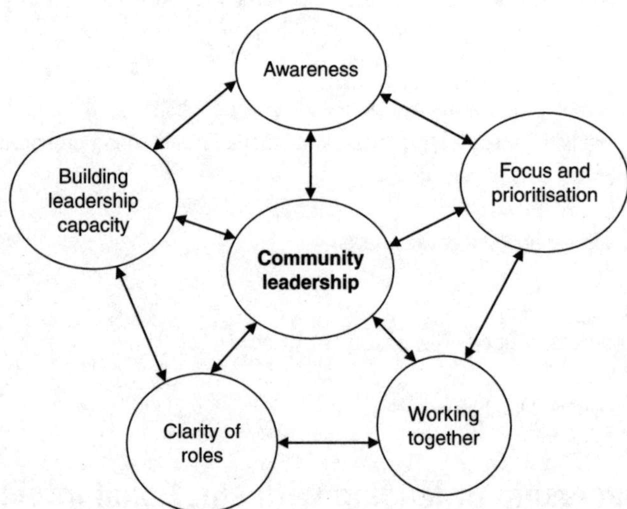

Source: Audit Commission analysis of corporate assessment reports

Community leadership does however raise a few questions for us. Most schools, children's centres and establishments are located in distinct communities but to what extent are they expected to be leaders? As we have seen the institutional definitions of community leadership tend to be drawn from organizations and institutions that are part of the overall democratic infrastructure, but we have to think through what is the nature of democracy and this can have implications for the way that we think about leadership. One of the critical questions around democracy is understanding the tension between having a representative democracy (whereby we elect our leaders in a secret ballot with universal suffrage) or a participative democracy (where we expect those who have power and authority over us to reference their decisions back to us, the follower for their approval). In society it is argued that we are moving towards a participative democracy where policies are – especially at a level around local services – constantly modified around the shifts in consumer needs. But maybe the line we have from central government is that we have a representative democracy in that we are in power until the next election and we have a mandate to carry on until we are forced to change.

These are important definitions that impact upon our implicit models of leadership. Take for instance the notion of choice that is being built into local services, the idea that we can have choice of local hospital, the choice of children's centre to send our children to or a choice of school. What is though the reality behind this? To have a choice of a place in a children's centre does in fact mean that we have to have two places vacant at any one time for someone to have a choice; we have to have two empty beds in different hospital wards and then where does this leave the agenda on efficiency? We think of leadership in much the same way, we want to have our followers and staff to have engagement and choice and to be participative, but there are times when you are the boss with the legitimacy to make choices and decisions on our behalf and you have to stand or fall by them. These ideas of community leadership are taking hold and will, we feel, have an increasing relevance for the leaders of services to children.

Leadership of place

Recently, an interesting departure in the direction of leadership research and thinking has emerged, that of leadership of place. The background to this comes from the developing understanding of what can make certain geographic locations more distinctive than others. One critical element of achieving that has been suggested is the political will of elected representatives to express their ambition for that particular geographical location as being uniquely differentiated from other places: giving expression to a town through encouraging a particular vernacular in architecture for instance. Another explanation is that a particular locality, such as a school is so strongly associated with one person, say a head teacher that that individual defines the place. Much of this theorizing is currently in its infancy but we feel that it has growing relevance for the audience we intend for this book.

Reflective task

Can you name a place that is so strongly associated with one person that any reference to that name will immediately mean that others know the place you are talking about?

Have you personal experience of any such locations – perhaps even from your own schooling?

What are your personal feelings about this? Do you see it as beneficial, or otherwise to think of a particular place being associated with any individual who might have had a significant impact upon that locality?

Leadership of place came out of the work on Community leadership and Local government leadership. The ten principles of place as outlined by Robert Hill (former No 10 advisor) are:

1. Places vary
2. Places have some needs in common
3. Places have history
4. Places in places matter
5. Places are multi-layered
6. Places are personal
7. Places can empower
8. Places can divide
9. Places need vision and leadership
10. Places need power to change things

(*Source*: Leadership Centre for Local Government 2006: 6)

Reflective task

Think about the locality you work in and the specific places. These might be school, children's centre, nursery or other early years setting. What is unique about this setting as a place? Then if you move out from the setting what are the key things that you would identify about the area? Use the ten principles to help you structure your thinking about your setting and the area in which it is situated.

Think about your key and critical stakeholders and find out about their perceptions of what is unique about your setting and the local area. Are there similarities and differences between the key people or groups involved?

Places need leaders

Joe Simpson (Leadership Centre for Local Government 2006) from the Leadership Centre has some advice for leaders about the key attributes needed for local leaders.

- Steering not rowing
- Commissioning and co-commissioning
- Influence not command and control

- Convening (and being convened)
- Thinking and acting long term
- Coping with complexity
- Listening and engaging
- Community mediation
- Vision (and storytelling)
- Strategic and community leadership

Although these are aimed at those working in local government and include political leaders you may see similarities in your own role in early years leadership within the list.

Features of successful leadership of place

Features of successful leadership of place have been identified from the Academy for Sustainable Communities (ASC) Study. This project involves research and the development of learning materials to build a better understanding of the strategic leadership challenges for economic development, planning and regeneration over the next decade (2006).

- Credible/authentic commitment to place
- 'Non-aligned' but engaged
- Clear and widely anchored vision: where are we trying to get to, why and how?
- Clear purpose: a sense of historical imperative: generational timescales
- Values: clear about what type of future
- Promotes a collective endeavour; pooling of resources (intellectual and material); reciprocity
- Promotes radical change agenda
- Importance of connecting all assets to gain 'whole' leverage
- Focus on people as *the* key asset; social capital
- Leadership as ongoing 'boundary mediation'
- Leadership as a process of 'continuous navigation' – rather than a time-limited or task-oriented mission
- Leadership teams that are configured for a particular/given developmental context
- Leadership that promotes a climate of *'No-Fuss-Learning'*

Although these are concepts that have now been around for some time, many would include 'visionary' and 'charismatic' leadership as being part of the new paradigms of leadership. Even though these conceptual leadership notions have been around for a few decades they have in recent times come under significant attack. While authors such as Jay Conger (1989) have promoted charismatic leadership in various forms others have questioned whether it is these idealized and individualized notions of leadership that have contributed to global strife?

Other new paradigm leadership researchers and commentators that remain prominent are House (1976) who championing the idea of visionary leadership has argued that one of the key determinants of effective leaders is that they have a compelling vision of the end state they are trying to create. Others such as Stacey (1996) have argued that although to have a vision for the organization or setting is vital it is too much of an unrealistic burden for this to be owned and developed by one person alone.

There are some interesting diversions appearing in the leadership research literature, for instance looking at leadership through the creation of environmental conditions. Influence is maintained through the leader creating or even manufacturing climates for others to operate in that determine high levels of morale and engagement.

As we have moved away from these at times 'heroic' notions of leadership it can be seen that at their heart are some very important concepts that still have relevance and meaning. Perhaps the most damming criticism is that the overwhelming basis of research that goes to support these theoretical stances on new paradigm models of leadership is that it is men who have studied other men to formulate these approaches, and to compound matters the research has been predominantly undertaken in white dominated societies. Perhaps we are just awakening to the fact the entire world might not be like this? Out there are other new paradigms of leadership that are awaiting the funding and motivation to be researched in depth to extend our thinking in leadership that is truly encompassing of the diverse world in which we now operate.

Summary of key ideas in this chapter

- Ideas about leadership are constantly changing as different contexts are explored.
- New paradigm approaches to leadership have increasingly attracted criticism – questions of how appropriate they are in a post 9/11 world and as to whether the pursuit of these notions of leadership have indeed contributed the current world state?
- Leadership in communities requires different kinds of leadership skills for leaders in the early years not just focused within one professional domain.
- Leadership of place is an important new area of study linked to the development of communities in a political climate for sustainability.
- Leadership of place is an important concept for children's centre leaders to explore further given the 'situatedness' of their leadership roles.

Further reading

Academy for Sustainable Communities (ASC) (2006). *Leadership of Place*. Leeds

Goleman, D., Boyatzis, R. and McKee, A. (2004). *Primal Leadership*. Harvard: HBS Press

Luft, J. and Ingham, H. (1955). 'The Johari window, a graphic model of interpersonal awareness', *Proceedings of the western training laboratory in group development*. Los Angeles: UCLA

Simon, H. (1991). Bounded Rationality and Organizational Learning, *Organization Science* 2(1): 125–134

Useful websites

http://www.ascskills.org.uk/pages/home

http://users.utu.fi/juhtiur/jakelu/monitahoarvio2.pdf for a research article about managerial self awareness in high performing individuals in organizations by Church (1997)

http://www.idea.gov.uk

http://www.localleadership.gov.uk/

All the above websites were last accessed on 21.09.08.

5 Leadership in Partnership

Chapter Outline

There are a number of current 'buzz' words used for partnerships in early years including multi-agency/multi-stake holder/multi-purpose. This chapter will assist you in exploring what these might mean and who this means you might be working alongside and within early years settings and why. It will also begin to explore the relationship between leading without line management responsibility for people.

Standards that this chapter will help you explore are:

Early Years: S33, S36

Social Care: Functional area A, Functional area B, Functional area C, Functional area D, Functional area E and Functional area F

Children's centre leaders: 1. Leading learning and development, 2. Stronger families, stronger communities, 4. Shaping the present and creating the future, 6. Building and strengthening teams

Teaching: Q5, Q6, Q32, C5, C6, C40, C41, P9, P10, E13, E14, E15, A2, A3, Shaping the future, Leading learning and teaching, developing self and working with others, Managing the organization, Securing accountability, Strengthening community

By the end of this chapter you will:

- have explored the different terms used in relation to partnership, multi-agency or multi-stakeholder working;
- have explored what it means to be leading in different kinds of partnerships;
- have explored some theoretical models that you can use to analysis partnership working.

Partnerships

Definitions of partnerships are varied and are often context specific. We will present you with a selection of definitions and ways of looking at partnerships that will give you a flavour of the variety.

Definitions

Nelson and Zadek (2000) looked at a variety of definitions. We have selected two different ones to explore in more detail here. The first is from the Ashridge Centre for Business and Society:

> Three or more organisations – representing the public, private and voluntary sector [*sic*] – acting together by contributing their diverse resources to pursue a common vision with clearly defined goals and objectives. The objective of a partnership should be to deliver more than the sum of the individual parts.

Secondly the Copenhagen Centre itself defines new social partnerships as follows:

> People and organisations from some combination of public, business and civil constituencies who engage in voluntary, mutually beneficial, innovative relationships to address common societal aims through combining their resources and competencies.

Characteristics

Sagawa and Segal (2000: 213–214) suggest that new value partnerships are characterized by several elements. We have created the acronym COMMON to describe these elements:

Common
Opportunity
Mutuality
Multiple levels
Open-endedness
New value

Bergquist et al. (1995: 18) focus on how partnership can extend the reach of an organization and this is an interesting and pertinent issue for early years settings like children's centres and their aim to engage hard to reach families. Bergquist et al. (1995: 10–18) offer six key rationales for partnerships.

1. Partnerships are often formed to yield *efficiency*. Partnerships allow participating organizations to do more with less. They provide high-quality products or services at lower costs than is possible working in isolation.
2. Partnerships provide *flexibility*. Their structures and agreements can readily be changed to meet shifting needs and conditions.
3. Partnerships offer *expanded resources*. Partners have easier, more convenient access to important specialized resources such as expertise, space, technology, and materials.
4. Partnerships often create *expanded markets* for their participating organizations, including a wider geographic reach and/or access to new segments of an established market.
5. Partnerships offer their participants a *sense of interdependence*. They offer connections and community, increasing their participants' involvement with and reliance on people in other participating organizations.
6. Partnerships offer an increased opportunity for *personal gratification*, including increased personal involvement, control, and professional fulfilment.

Partnerships and value

Doz and Hamel (1998: xv) explored the relationship between partnerships and value. They focus on the management of the partnership and the fact that there is usually a dominant partner who takes on the management role. This highlights the importance of having partnership agreements in place before any work is undertaken. Preparatory work is needed before partnership working can start effectively.

'To date, most intercompany collaborations have involved the setting up and management of joint ventures in well-circumscribed areas. In most areas, these ventures are designed to contain and share known risks, not to create an expansive future. These risks are well understood, and the strategic foundations of the joint venture are clear to the partners, whose managers focus most of their attention on the economics and contractual design of the agreement. Once agreement is reached, one of the partners usually assumes operating responsibility and, for all practical purposes, runs the operation as if it were the sole owner. This arrangement lacks the dynamism, collaboration and mutual learning characteristic of successful strategic alliances.' The strategic alliance, in contrast, is characterized by the following:

- There is greater uncertainty and ambiguity.
- The manner in which value is created – and the way in which partners capture it – is not preordained.
- The partner relationship evolves in ways that are hard to predict.

- Today's ally may be tomorrow's rival – or may be a current rival in some other market.
- Managing the alliance relationship over time is usually more important than crafting the initial formal design.
- Initial agreements have less to do with success than does adaptability to change.

Reflective task

Existing leaders

Although these selections might at first appear very business dominated which of these perspectives do you think makes how your organization sees partnership working?

Aspiring leaders

Which of these perspectives do you think you would want to aspire to using as a leader and why?

Multi-agency working

The ideas of multi-agency working across organizations might appear to be a new notion in relation to leadership, but it is an area that has been around for a considerable amount of time. The terms used to describe the key ideas may be different, but the focus remains the same. The principle is about the coming together of organizations to deliver together. If you think about the supply of gas to your home for example this involves a number of different groups of people employed by different organizations to get the supply of gas from the original source to you as the customer. Each member of the groups of people has a specific function and brings with them expertise and/or resources to the work, and there is a clear focus for their combined work that is the supply of gas to customers. They will have drawn up agreements about how they will work together and the parameters of each member of the groups work. If these organizations worked in isolation it would be difficult for them to achieve the gaol of providing services and for the originations to make a profit for any shareholders. Within public services the notions of not needing to make a profit has been seen as not only a key difference between private and public services but also as a rationale for seeing the two as almost completely separate entities and therefore anything written about private organizations could not be applied in any way to any public services.

In the area of children's services the Every Child Matters (DfES 2004a) agenda with the five outcomes

- Be healthy
- Stay safe
- Enjoy and achieve
- Make a positive contribution
- Achieve economic well-being

has become the key focus for all those providing services for children. For public, private, voluntary and independent organizations it gives a clear picture of what is to be achieved and provides a shared language with which people can discuss between organizations about what they can bring to any local group of organizations offering services to children and their families. In addition to working across organizations this means that people working with children and families will come from different professional backgrounds.

Frost (2005) offers definitions to characterize the continuum of partnership working.

Multi-disciplinary individuals or a team from different agencies who

- Cooperate – services work to together towards consistent goals and complementary services while maintaining their independence.
- Collaborate – services plan and address issues of overlap, duplication and gaps in service provision towards common outcomes.
- Coordination – services work together in a planned manner towards shared and agreed goals.
- Merger/integration – different services become an organization in order to enhance service delivery.
- Joined-up – refers to overcoming existing professional and institutional barriers that impede seamless or even adequate services to families and communities.

Within some organizations co-location of services is seen as the answer to encouraging people to work together but if you have ever been into a classroom and seen children sitting around a table together this doesn't mean that they are automatically working together they may be simply sitting at the same table but all working independently. The same can be seen with adults if you have been to a conference or course and carrying out activities you may not have engaged with others partly as a result of not knowing people and partly as a result of the activities you have been given do not encourage you to work with others.

There are important lessons here for multi-agency working as the quality of the relationships between any partners and their individual members are crucial to establishing the most effective working relationships. As in establishing the trust in small groups/teams in one organization the same is true of larger groupings. We need to understand the role each of the partners play within the relationship, what they will bring to the relationship and how this links to our own purpose, skills and knowledge. It may not always appear obvious what each organization can offer to the total package of services for children and families in a specific locality.

Reflective task

For this task you will need to use your experience of working with people from different agencies and different professional backgrounds. If you are just starting out this will be your opportunity to find out about the range of people who are working within children's services and what they might bring to any partnership arrangement. Try to fill out the following chart and include yourself in this as your own background and experiences are important as you would be/are part of the team.

Title of role	Organization that they work for	Qualifications and training	Main focus of their work with children and families	Where most of their work is carried out	Usual partners

We have deliberately included title of role and how this may differ from what they actually do as sometimes titles can be misleading and also hold preconceived notions from our own past experiences. We are not focusing on the leadership standards that might directly apply to each profession, but you might also find it useful when you have finished filling in the chart to return to Chapter 1 and compare the leadership requirements based on professional backgrounds. If you are already working in an early years setting you may find this exercise helpful to share with your team so they begin to see what everyone brings to the setting and working with children and their families.

Leading people for whom you have no line management responsibility

One big issue that people have in relation to leading people in partnership arrangements is the relationship between leadership and line management. Do you always need to have line management for people you lead? The answer is no you don't, but it takes getting used to the fact that you may have no authority over a persons work event though they are based in your setting and this is where they carry out the majority of their work. This is real leadership as you cannot rely on a management position and its association authority to give a direction to their work. Tasks need to be negotiated rather than given as orders. You can share a vision for the setting together and share an understanding of the expectations of their work with adults and children in the setting. The same person may have supervision and appraisal sessions outside the setting and event their professional development. People come together to work in partnership because they are working on the same project.

Reflective task

Within the setting you work in or a setting you know find out about all the people who work with children and their families in the setting. Find out who these people work for and why they are part of the staffing for the setting. Do they offer specialist skills? Find out about the shared vision for the setting and how everyone has agreed this.

Distance and distribution

Armstrong and Cole (2002) have focused their research 'Managing Distances and Differences in Geographically Distributed Work Groups' and have found that identification is a person's sense of belonging within a social category. This 'identification' in virtual organizational teams is thought to be especially desirable because it provides the glue that can promote group cohesion despite the relative lack of face-to-face interaction. Though research on virtual teams is exploding, it has not systematically identified the antecedents or moderators of the process by which identification develops, leaving a number of gaps and apparent contradictions. Their work explores the contradictions and addresses some of the gaps by tracing the mechanisms and moderating processes through which identification develops in hybrid and pure virtual settings, and the ways that these processes differ from face-to-face settings. This is a particularly important piece of work for the kinds of multi-agency, multi-professional work now expected of early years setting especially children's centres where outreach work and/or activities take place in a range of situations and are not concentrated in a specific hub or centre where the people who carry out the work do not necessarily meet together on a regular basis and communication is via email, telephone calls or notes. The form of communication is a potential source of misinterpretation or confusion unless the identities within the group are clearly established.

Reflective task

Current leader

Consider how communication is carried out across the range of partners in your organization and how people are made to feel part of the team. What are the advantages and disadvantages of the systems used? How might you improve these?

Aspiring leader

Consider how communication is carried out in a setting. Talk to members of the team who are there all the time and if you can, talk to people who only work within the functions of the setting for a small part of their working week. What are the differences that they express about the communication within and outside the organization?

Agreement and certainty matrix

Ralph Stacey (1996) developed a matrix as a method to select the appropriate management actions in a complex adaptive system based on the *degree of certainty* and *level of agreement* on the issue in question.

Close to certainty	Issues or decisions are close to certainty when cause and effect linkages can be determined. This is usually the case when a very similar issue or decision has been made in the past. You can then extrapolate from past experience to predict the outcome of an action with a good degree of certainty.
Far from certainty	At the other end of the certainty continuum are decisions that are far from certainty. These situations are often unique or at least new to the decision makers. The cause and effect linkages are not clear. Extrapolating from past experience is not a good method to predict outcomes in the far from certainty range.
Agreement	The vertical axis measures the level of agreement about an issue or decision within the group, team or organization. As you would expect, the management or leadership function varies depending on the level of agreement surrounding an issue.

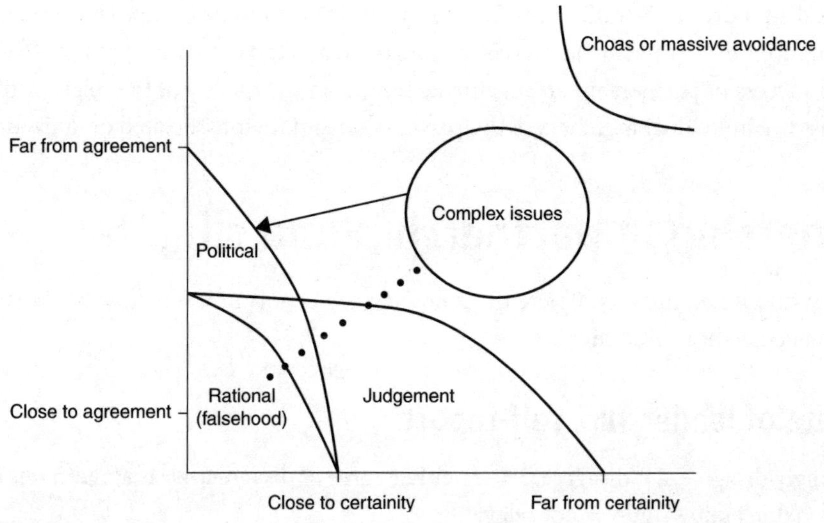

Source: Stacey (1996: 177–180)

In complex organizations like early years settings including Children's centres leaders are expected to operate in partnerships where there may not be agreement about services, finances or priorities for work. Leaders are also expected to be able to operate in the political field, which although it might appear that they should be working towards a rational solution to issues this can sometimes produce a falsehood or false picture of the complex situation.

Old ideas revisited

With her concern for creative experience, democracy and for developing local community organizations, Mary Parker Follett is an often forgotten, but still deeply instructive thinker for educators and community developers.

With her concern for creative experience, democracy and for developing local community organizations, Mary Parker Follett is an often forgotten, but still deeply instructive thinker for educators and social animateurs.

> The training for the new democracy must be from the cradle – *through nursery, school and play, and on and on through every activity of our life. Citizenship is not to be learned in good government classes or current events courses or lessons in civics. It is to be acquired only through those modes of living and acting which shall teach us how to grow the social consciousness. This should be the object of all day school education, of all night school education, of all our supervised recreation, of all our family life, of our club life, of our civic life.* (Mary Parker Follett 1918: 363)

She looked to approach organizations as group networks rather than as hierarchical structures, and attended to the influence of human relations within the group. These are key ideas for the notions of partnership across early years provision today. So much of the effectiveness and the success of partnership arrangements hinges on the quality of the relationships built up across the individual members of the partnership and their associated organizations.

Leadership in partnership and climate

You may find it helpful to complete the following self-report to assess how ready you are to work in partnership with others.

Climate of leadership, self-report

1 = strongly disagree, 2 = disagree, 3 = is neither agree or disagree, 4 = is agree, 5 = is strongly agree, x = don't know and y = not relevant.

		1	2	3	4	5	x	y
1	I attempt to display a positive concern for the well-being, development of others while maintaining positive expectations of them.							
2	I try to communicate the future strategy and vision for others and maintain the support of others inside and outside the organization.							
3	I attempt to ensure that others trust me and try to delegate activities appropriately where I can.							
4	I try to put personal ambition behind the good of others.							
5	I am open to criticism and accept others have a different view of the world.							
6	I try to reduce the negative impact of status and to always engage others in a face-to-face manner.							
7	I can make decisions, even when difficult and communicate them to all in the team and organization.							

		1	2	3	4	5	x	y
8	I will take time to clarify the boundaries between what I do and others and keep others informed of what I am doing.							
9	I have a very clear vision for the future and invite others to contribute to the development of this vision.							
10	I generally have a positive impact on others' motivation and work to inspire others to join me.							
11	I work to avoid joining cliques and power groups.							
12	I encourage others to question my personal performance and to give me feedback.							
13	I am not critical of others mistakes and avoid apportioning blame when things do not go the way I want.							
14	I have a high level of creativity and intellectual versatility when I have to solve problems.							
15	I avoid the use of jargon and am non-judgemental in interpersonal communications.							
16	I am accessible and visible to others at all levels and am concerned communicating issues quickly and free from bias.							
17	I both welcome feedback and act upon it wherever it comes from.							
18	I avoid the use of position and status.							
19	I can communicate to people at all levels, inside and outside the organization without compromising my personal integrity.							
20	I make time to balance the interests of staff, the team, the organization and stakeholders.							

80–100 = intention to create excellence climate for partnerships
79–50 = working towards the creation of a climate for collaborative partnerships
49–0 = seek advise and support to enable you to begin to develop the climate for partnerships
More than 5 x or y's consider development opportunities like being mentored or shadowing existing leaders in strong partnership settings.

Summary of key ideas in this chapter

- leadership of partnerships is not an easy area
- leadership of partnerships is a complex area
- for partnerships to work well each member needs to feel part of the organization regardless of the distance from any hub centre of services
- the quality of the relationships between the people in the partnership determines the effectiveness of the working relationship

Further reading

Armstrong, D. J. and Cole, P. (2002). Managing Distances and Differences in Geographically Distributed Work Groups. In P. Hinds, and S. Kiesler (Eds), *Distributed Work* (pp. 167–186). Massachusetts Institute of Technology

Sagawa, S. and Segal, E. (2000). Common Interest Common Good: Creating Value Through Business and Social Sector Partnerships. Harvard Business School Press

Stacey, R. D. (1996). *Complexity and Creativity in Organizations.* San Francisco: Berrett-Koehler Publishers

Useful websites

Every child matters leadership direct can be found at http://www.ncsl.org.uk/priorities-index/priorities-ecmleadershipdirect.htm

http://www.childrens-centres.org/default.aspx

http://www.direct.gov.uk/en/index.htm

http://www.kingsfund.org.uk/leadership/index.html for ideas about leadership from a health perspective

http://www.scie.org.uk/ for the Social Care Institute for Excellence

All the above websites were last accessed on 21.09.08.

The Range of Leadership Challenges in the Early Years

6

Chapter Outline

This chapter looks at the range of leadership challenges for those working in the early years through case studies of leaders in difference circumstances. It is not possible to cover all the potential different routes into early years leadership but the vignettes here will give you a flavour not only of the individual's challenges, but also how those working with them may perceive their backgrounds and how they themselves perceive their backgrounds. You may as you read these find elements that apply to you in more than one of the vignettes or you may identify with a specific professional background. You will find that most of the case studies here are portrayed as female and this reflects the majority of the workforce in this field. Each vignette is drawn from a number of people's experiences and backgrounds rather than from a single person, and they also draw upon the most positive aspects of these leadership roles in different early years settings.

Standards that this chapter will help you explore are:

Early Years: S33, S34, S35, S36

Social Care: Functional area A, Functional area B, Functional area C, Functional area D, Functional area E and Functional area F

⇨

Children's centre leaders: 1. Leading learning and development, 2. Stronger families, stronger communities, 3. Being accountable and responsible, 4. Shaping the present and creating the future, 5. Managing the organization, 6. Building and strengthening teams

Teaching: Q5, Q6, Q32, Q33, C5, C6, C40, C41, P9, P10, E13, E14, E15, A2, A3, Shaping the future, Leading learning and teaching, Developing self and working with others, Managing the organisation, Securing accountability, Strengthening community

By the end of this chapter you will:

- have an appreciation of the different professional backgrounds people might have while still being a leader in the early years;
- have explored some of the issues a specific background may create for those in leadership roles;
- know how leaders might perceive their own experiences and professional backgrounds;
- have different ways of working with others who have different kinds of expertise;
- have considered the challenges of leadership and power;
- have explored the challenges of poor and good performance in the workplace.

Reflective task

Before you begin to read the series of short vignettes in this chapter try writing down the different roles and professional backgrounds that people working in the early years might have and keep the list to compare at the end of reading this chapter. Also write down the types of settings that early years practitioners might work in.

Kinds of settings

Children's centres

According to the Surestart website children's centres are 'service hubs where children under five years old and their families can receive seamless integrated services and information' (Surestart.gov.uk 2008). By 2010 every community in the country should have access to a centre's provision. Part of these services may be local day care provision, crèches, stay and plays or other locally determined early years provision.

Foundation stage units

These are found most often in primary, first or infant schools where children are grouped together across the nursery and reception age group of 3–5 although you may find some settings which include younger children and some where the unit includes children through into year one (six-year-olds). The organization of the setting can vary and sometimes there are spaces to which all children have access all of the time but have bay or group areas for registration and more structured teaching slots in the day. Children are usually allocated to a specific adult in the unit who acts as a key worker and liases with parents and carers.

Nurseries

This term covers a wide range of different types of settings from an LA (Local Authority)-run nursery school through private, voluntary and community run care for children from 0–5.

Schools

Schools, that is depending upon where you live primary (3–11 or 4–11), infant (3–7 or 4–7) or first (3–8, 4–8 or 3–9 or 4–9) schools have reception classes for 4/5-year-olds-and some have nurseries attached or nursery classes offering part or full education for 3/4-year-olds within the state system.

Pre-school playgroups

These are mainly groups running for children between the ages of 2–4 on a sessional basis of between 2–4 hours every day or for several weeks a year. They're run on a not-for-profit basis (so they're not state or private), most often by parent management committees but supported by organizations like the Pre-school Learning Alliance (PLA).

The Professionals

Each of these people are leading either a whole organization or a specific strand of the early years provision which draws upon their professional backgrounds and expertise.

The head teacher

The leader in this case study has focused on early years throughout her teaching career but now has broadened her experience as the primary school she is head of has children's centre status. Her strengths have been working with young children and their families from an educational starting point. She is used to working with other agencies particularly with children with special educational needs and additional needs such as looked after children. Locally the school is seen as a resource for support for parents and the head is seen as someone who listens to and spends time with families when it is needed. The challenges for leadership for this head are around the perceptions of other professionals providing services for the children's centre. For some she is just seen as a teacher and therefore has little or no knowledge of other services and other professions, as this has previously not been an expectation of her role. This view is difficult to work with as the head does not want to be seen as trying to be an expert in everything as this could be seen as arrogance yet she needs people from other professional heritages to know she is aware of the value of different professionals expertise and working together everyone can benefit.

Other challenges are around the quality of provision for young children in education and care situations. As a trained teacher the head has expectations about adult and child interactions, use of resources with a focus on children's learning.

The administrator/finance leader

This children's centre leader has come from a finance background, which may appear to be a strange route into working with young children yet this person brings significant organizational skills to the role. For a number of years their finance role was within the Local authority so they are well aware of the procedures used by the managing organization and this has been helpful for the centre in knowing who to talk to and how to present information using the correct systems. Initially and partly because of this person's background they focused on management or transactional leadership and were seen as getting things completed. This was an important function as the children's centre was first established, dealing with builders for a new purpose built centre and organization of the appointment of staff and clearly managing the budget. As the centre developed the challenge for this leader was to focus more on the people within the centre and developing their work and less about the systems and structures, which support the running of the organization. The latter were in place and agreed swiftly because of the leadership style of the individual.

The private nursery owner leader

This nursery owner has been approached to be part of the core offer for a children's centre as the centre is not in a position to offer full day care as an integral part of the centre. The nursery owner is keen to be involved in the services for children and families in the locality but doesn't have any knowledge of children's centres or working in a multi-agency environment. She has a childcare background and is keen to continue to improve the facilities in the nursery and attract high quality staff and obviously fee-paying parents. She has recently registered to complete her 'Early Years Professional status' (EYPS) qualification. Her challenges are to become more familiar with the children's centre agenda and to find out what this would mean for her business. She is about to take some soundings from parents who currently use the nursery and to talk to her staff.

The health professional leader

This leader is working in a children's centre, which is managed for the local authority by the PCT (Primary Care Trust) for whom the leader works. She has a background as a health visitor and so the integration of health services including midwives, health visitors and some doctor's services is strength of the provision. There is a private contractor offering day care on the premises, but it has been hard to negotiate having places in the nursery available for restbite care for families or odd sessions for doctors appointments for example. Liaison with local schools has been more difficult as roles are falling and all schools have nursery classes, and therefore the day care has been seen as competition for the schools.

The community worker leader

The community worker in this example is a local man who has worked for many years in developing community projects and has worked for a National charity, which has taken on the running of children's centres in the area. The children's centre where the community worker is based has a day care facility in a separate location, which has been offering day care for some time and has a stable staff group. The community worker has experience of youth and adult community work but no experience of working with young children. One area for his development is how can he get involved in the day care and what strategies he employs to work on the quality of the provision. His leadership style is not directive and staff don't always know what is expected yet he sees himself as giving them autonomy in their daily roles.

The social worker leader

The social worker in this example came from working specifically with children and young people with disabilities and therefore had experience of dealing with integration into the education system of children and young people with specific needs. They also had experience of working within social care teams and supervision of casework especially with safeguarding children. For this professional the challenges are around the protocols for sharing information about children and families and working with other professionals as potential lead professionals in the CAF (Common Assessment Framework) process.

The early years professional leader

This early years professional has completed her EYPS and is working in a voluntary funded and managed nursery facility. She has experience across the early years age range but has spent most of her time with the under threes. The majority of her work is directly with the children and she has limited access to parents and carers as they tend to drop their children off at sessions and then leave for work or other activities. The voluntary organization wishes to move to provide other services to families and their children and wants to encourage nursery staff to be involved in this process. As an EYP this professional has a leadership role in relation to the quality of provision for children and working with other members of the team to develop practice. She sees herself as being a specialist providing leadership for a small area of the total provision by the organization and therefore a big challenge for her is seeing the 'bigger picture' of the organization as a whole.

The foundation stage teacher

This professional has come straight through a teaching training and has spent a number of years teaching across the Foundation stage. They have a specific leadership role for the staff and children across the Foundation stage and this includes liaison with feeder nurseries, pre-schools and playgroups in the area. As teacher training concentrates on threes and over this professional has had limited experience of working with the under threes and direct work with families outside an educational focus. She sees herself as being a specialist providing leadership early years education within the school and therefore a big challenge for her is seeing the 'bigger picture' of the provision for families and children in the local area and beginning to work more closely with other agencies.

Speech and language therapist

This professional has very specialist knowledge, and she is passionate about developing young children's language skills. She has been working with a health visitor running a course for parents and carers about talking to their children from birth to improve communication skills in both adults and children. She is employed by the local PCT (Primary Care Trust) who want her to concentrate on the referrals through the health clinics. She would like to work in a more inclusive way with other professionals as she has done with the health visitor. He challenge is convincing her line manager of the benefits of a different way of working.

Early years teacher working in children's centres

This professional has come straight through a teaching training and has spent a number of years teaching across the Foundation stage and then working in nurseries to gain her EYPS. She has decided to work in children's centres as she wants to focus on the quality of activities offered for children to enhance their cognitive development and make a difference to their life chances later. She has a specific leadership role education under 'enjoying and achieving', across a number of children's centres and this includes liaison with nurseries, pre-schools and playgroups in the area. As teacher training concentrates on threes and over this professional had limited experience of working with the under threes until completing her EYPS. She also has had little opportunity for direct work with families outside an educational focus. Her challenge is persuading other professionals in the children's centre that she has experiences and knowledge to share to develop activities for children without staff feeling as though she is criticizing their current practice.

Reflective task

Look again at your list of people working in the early years in different types of leadership positions. How did your list compare with those offered in this chapter? Were there any surprises for you? Were you aware of the wide range of people who you might come into contact with working in this field?

Make a note of some of the roles and/or professional backgrounds you would like to find out more about.

Leadership and personal power

Power in leadership settings is not unidirectional, the staff are not powerless and the leader Omni powerful; power is a question of balance but the power that one person has over another or group of others needs to be carefully thought through as to where the sources of power lie. Also, it may be that as leaders we draw our power from one source or even a multiplicity of sources that could be contingent upon the circumstances we are in. For instance, when you as a leader are in the company of your manager (as your nearby leader) do you exercise your personal power in a different way as to when you are alone with a member of staff. This may be a very uncomfortable idea, but our behaviour, attitude and orientation to others will be influenced by the sources of power we draw as leaders.

There are a number of sources of power

Positional power – the power that comes from occupying a specific role in a hierarchy or system. To make this legitimate it must be endorsed by the wider structure and values system you operate in.

Personal power – drawn from your values that drive your orientation, if you are personally highly committed to a scenario or a particular vision you will become identified with it and accrue power to yourself as a leader as a result of this.

Reward power – you can satisfy the needs of others with rewards. These can be on the surface very minor rewards – an acknowledgement for work well done, a respectful thank you or they can in certain circumstances be power invested in you to offer rewards for others' efforts.

Coercive power – you create compliance through arousing fear in others, this could be through contingent use of rules and procedures or through making others feel guilty for what they have done.

Enabling power – how you empower others to resolve issues and conflicts.

Expert power – the power you have from high levels of expertise and experience – having done things before you have expert power.

Information power – the ability you have to access information that others require.

Resource power – the access you have to resources that are restricted to others, not just budgetary and financial resources but also the resource of time and discretion.

Associative powers – power you have through your access to networks and alliances that you have created or are part of.

Labelling power – the power you have to achieve a focus on important priorities that others also identify with.

What is vital to this is that you may have a combination of sources of power dependent upon where you are situated in a system and that at any time the sources of power you draw upon is dynamic. Even within a formal meeting you may as an effective leader move between various sources of power as you bring influence to leaders. Also, those whom you lead may have an expectation of you to draw on certain types of power at certain times. An example might be when dealing with an awkward customer, a mixture of expert and positional power might be appropriate.

Reflective task

Existing leaders

Go to your diary and pick a particularly busy day when you recently interacted with lots of people in various meetings. Go through that day and map the sources of power you drew upon.

When you have done this look for a day in the future where you again will have a great deal of interaction with others and think what sources of power you, as a leader will draw upon to make those exchanges as effective as possible.

Think through a time when you worked for a boss and try and map out what sources of power they may have had a preference for using with you.

Aspiring leaders

Go to your diary and pick a particularly busy day when you recently interacted with lots of people in various ways whether during your studies, work or social time. Go through that day and map the sources of power you drew upon.

How have you used your power in situations to influence decisions from who would scribe in a group task to where you would go for the evening out?

These are the same kinds of power that you would draw upon as a leader in a setting, and it is worth being aware of the power and influence you have already before taking up a leader's position.

Key points from this section

It is hard to envisage any notion of leadership where the leader is powerless.

Leaders can maximize their positive impact upon others through a careful and reflective awareness of the behaviours they display drawn from the power sources they may be applying.

Ineffective or even highly destructive leaders may be naive in the power sources they rely on and may not recognize that it is contingent upon the circumstances they are in.

For you as a leader, are there times when you may draw upon less than satisfactory sources of power?

Issues of leadership and the performance of others

One of the key drivers for organizations and even governments to invest in leadership development for senior staff is the perceived impact improved leadership has on staff and therefore organizational performance; individual mangers are however often keen to develop their subordinate managers and leaders to enable them to deal with poor or less than desirable performance in their staff. This is irrespective as to whether there is any real evidence of poor performance. Often poor, or less than desirable performance is confused with staff appearing to be less than fully committed to the direction the organization is taking at a corporate level. Nevertheless there are consistent issues around poor performance.

One of the key areas that managers in senior strategic positions often fail to explore is the leadership impact of their subordinate leaders. They can often judge others leadership in a distorted way and seek evidence from sources that are not always about leadership. There are cases where strategic leaders have looked to evidence their investment in leadership development of subordinate managers in immediate improvements in outputs or by lack or profitability or productivity. This may be because they are confusing management with leadership.

To help unravel this let's think again as to what are the dividing lines between leadership and management. Management we have argued is about getting the job done, it is about the impact a person has on a system and the attainment of measurable organization objectives, but leadership is much more about the positive motivational impact one individual has on others or groups of others, therefore, if we are looking for evidence of improved leadership we ought to look more closely at some of the more measurable outcomes we have around motivation and a sense of well-being that staff feel while at work. Many organizations and early years institutions are looking at the growing application of staff attitude and climate surveys – many corporate institutions now rely on them quite heavily. We need to exercise an element of care over these as they can often be incorrectly interpreted; managers and professionals alike can lead to the creation of a belief that the results of attitude surveys provide an empirical and true measure of what is going on in a setting or whole organization. What they actually deliver for us is 'indicative' data that is useful when it is treated as such and used to help us ask more detailed and targeted questions of staff. Many examples exist of organizations using outputs from climate and staff surveys as tools to beat managers over the head with – asking why has this year's survey led to a 5 per cent decrease in satisfaction? We dig a bit deeper though; sometimes staff can report levels of dissatisfaction as a product of being made aware of issues for instance. If a leader is concerned with improving morale in a team then discussions about morale can lead to staff reporting lower levels of morale within the team as it is an issue that is being talked about and as a result high expectations become even higher. This in turn can and does in our experience lead to many confused situations where senior leaders can be left with a false feeling of poor performance where it does not exist in reality. We do not however deny that dealing with poor performance in staff is not a difficult and challenging issue to deal with, rather we just encourage the exercising of caution over the roots of poor performance as in many cases what seems to be is not is how it is in reality!

The leader and poor performance

Reflective task

Just take a few moments and think about a person who you have worked with whose performance has been an issue for you.

Think about how much you knew personally about what inspired that poor performer, what issues and circumstances would lead to a positive response from them?

Think about what you know about what caused them to be highly engaged and motivated?

If the person you were thinking of was a member of your staff ponder this for a moment.

Perceptions of poor performers

In 2008 Watson Wyatt, a highly respected consulting firm looked at what perceptions poor performers had of their nearby leaders, the results are startling:

Less than a third of poor performers,

Felt their nearby leader was effective at communicating their expectations of them, either in terms of their work/task outputs or personally of their behaviour, attitude and orientation to their work;

Felt their nearby leader was poor at establishing and agreeing goals for them to achieve and;

Felt that their nearby leader was unable to provide clear and unambiguous feedback to them on their individual performance.

In addition to the above, less than 30 per cent of the identified poor performers who were polled felt that their manager (or nearby leader) was able to link their performance to the performance of the team or organization nor were they able to link it to the rewards they received at work.

All this means is that dealing with poor performers at work is much more complicated than just finding a way of exiting from their jobs. Also, better management is not always the answer to dealing with poor performance; the Watson Wyatt work underscores that it is leadership impact and the effective positive motivational influence on others that is the better potential route to dealing with less than adequate performance.

Acknowledging good performance

Unfortunately we tend to dwell upon the negatives of performance and although we might sometimes recognize that people have completed jobs, activities or other elements of their work well this is not always acknowledged. Gaining not feedback except the negative kind can lead to feelings of being picked on or singled out. It can also lead to frustration with the lack of knowledge regarding expectations. These in turn can lead to increases in absences from work or other performance issues. It can make staff feel that they have no support from the management of the organization. At best we tend to assume that we are doing 'alright' unless someone tells us otherwise.

Reflective task

When was the last time you received positive feedback on any aspect of your life including work?

When was the last time you gave someone positive feedback about something they had done in any aspect of your life including work?

Focusing on the positive aspects of performance links with behaviour management policies with children in the early years where we emphasize the good behaviours rather than the negative ones.

How do we say well done?

'*While money is important to employees, what tends to motivate them to perform and to perform at higher levels is the thoughtful, personal kind of recognition that signifies true appreciation for a job well done.' Nelson (1997)*

We all want to know when we are doing a good job. When leaders recognize good performance it confirms to someone the accuracy and value of their work; your praise tells a person that you appreciate their efforts, which motivates them to work with you and other team members in the future. It makes people want to succeed. When acknowledging someone's performance you should mention the quality of the results they have accomplished as well as the effort they invested. It is worth being specific. Tell the person exactly what they did or produced that you appreciate. Provide your feedback promptly after the event so it acknowledges when work is completed not a long time afterwards as this can lesson the effects of the praise.

Some ways in which you might consider giving feedback on good performance

Complete a 'Notice of Outstanding Work Performance' or similar kind of award.

Send a member of staff a handwritten note or even an email as a record for themselves and any portfolio of evidence they might be asked to collect as part of the appraisal process.

Say 'Thank You' when a member of staff has done well.

Acknowledge a member of staff and their work in a public setting, a team meeting for example. Make sure that they are comfortable with public acknowledgement first though or you intentions will not be seen as positively as you would like.

Complete performance reviews and provide examples of positive performance along with examples of what needs to be improved.

When acknowledging a member of staff's achievements it is worth remembering the following:

Give immediate feedback or acknowledgment.

Be specific about the member of staff's job performance. Explain what they did well or what needs improvement.

Praise should be given when a member of staff goes above and beyond what is expected.

Don't acknowledge one member of staff when a group is responsible for the outcome as this can create resentment among the group and lead to poor performance with future activities.

Don't always single out one person. This can create competition among staff.

Reflective task

Consider how you might improve giving positive feedback to others with whom you work. Remember to consider all categories of staff in the work place including line managers.

Summary of key ideas in this chapter

- early years provision takes place in a wide range of different settings
- there are a wide range of professionals with different experiences and backgrounds all leading aspects of early years provision
- leadership has a direct impact on the performance of others working within the setting
- leadership has an impact on the quality of the provision of services for children and their families.
- we must acknowledge that leaders have power and draw this from a range of sources
- we need to acknowledge good and poor performance for staff, ourselves and our line managers

Further reading

Muijs, D., Aubrey, C., Harris, A. and Briggs, M. (2005). How do they manage? A review of the research on leadership in early childhood. *Journal of Early Childhood Research*. 2(2), 157–169

Nelson, B. (1997). *1001 Ways to Reward Employees*. New York: Workman Publishing Company

Watson Wyatt (2008). *Poor Leadership in Motivating Poorer-Performing Staff*.

http://www.hrmguide.co.uk/performance/poor-leadership.htm

Useful websites

http://www.surestart.gov.uk/

http://www.teachernet.gov.uk

http://www.scie.org.uk/

http://www.kingsfund.org.uk/leadership/index.html

http://www.networks.nhs.uk

All the above websites were last accessed on 21.09.08.

7 Planning the Development of Your Own Leadership Skills

Chapter Outline

Standards that this chapter will help you explore are:

Early Years: S33, S34, S35, S36
Social Care: Functional area A, Functional area B, Functional area C, Functional area D, Functional area E and Functional area F
Children's centre leaders: 1. Leading learning and development, 3. Being accountable and responsible, 4. Shaping the present and creating the future
Teaching: Q5, Q6, Q32, Q33, C5, C6, C40, C41, P9, P10, E13, E14, E15, A2, A3, Shaping the future, Leading learning and teaching, Developing self and working with others, Managing the organization, Securing accountability, Strengthening community

By the end of this chapter you will:

- have audited your current skills and experiences
- have considered the importance of the context of your leadership development

- have explored what a genuine concern for others means
- have considered the use of metaphor for describing your leadership development
- have explored your personal approach to leadership development
- have explored different types of leadership development opportunities and their advantages and disadvantages
- have explored 360 instruments in more detail

Auditing your current skills and experiences

Look back at the standards in the Appendix of Professional Standards that are the closest fit to your role, or the role to which you aspire in the introduction and see if you can fill in the following matrix.

The importance of the context for your leadership development

A key element of leadership in organizations is to be aware of the implications of the size of the organization and this we feel, is a key element to those working in the settings around children's services and schools. Those who work in larger organizations dominate any review of the literature around leadership from the period up to the mid-1980s. Popular literature and articles published tend to still emphasize the role of business leaders in large organization – can you think why this might be?

When we think of people as effective leaders we often have very different expectations of those who are socially close to us as opposed to the heroes and heroines who sit at he head of corporate organizations.

Reflective task

Just pause for a moment and think about what your expectation is of the Chief Executive Officer of the local authority where you either live or work. This will be an organization of many thousand staff, even for the smallest local authority – then think for a moment about the person to whom you report.

What different expectations do you have of these people?
Why might you have different expectations?
Think about the amount of time you may spend in their company?
Think about the settings in which you might come into contact with them?
Think about the roles they perform – what are the differences?

Standards	Evidence from activities/ events including experiences	Documentary evidence e.g. meetings, assignments, reports written, agendas	Evidence from reflective diary or notebook	Evidence from colleagues e.g. informal feedback	Evidence from formal systems including supervisions, appraisal, performance management	Any other sources of evidence	Comments, issues and other notes

Why is it then if you find certain differences is the majority of leadership research focused upon the Chief Executive roles as leaders?

This issue is we feel one of the most significant for anyone who is serious about the their own personal leadership development. Modelling leadership behaviours on those who are in remote and distant positions has massive implications for those in leadership roles where the span of control is more limited than in large complex organizations – this is not to say that we think that many of the settings in which the readership of this text are located is not complex – rather than the behaviours distinctly dependent upon who is to be engaged by the individual leader.

When thinking about leadership development it is now essential to differentiate between being a 'distant' leader and a 'nearby' leader.

A useful way to help you make this differentiation is for you to think back to your own school days. The best class teachers we tend to have were the ones that we felt we had a relationship with, ones that inspired us and encouraged us to think about the work we were doing in class. The head teacher we felt often played a very different role in our minds as pupils in this school. Many saw the head teacher as an authority figure, and we had a different learning relationship with that individual.

One key element of this is to think about the amount of time we spent with the class teacher as opposed to the head teacher, the visibility of the distant leader was less than the class teacher as our nearby leader.

Reflective task

Can you think of any other settings where we make this differentiation?

Can you think of the occasions when others make the distinction with you in the roles that you perform?

If you work in a larger organization say a school or children's centre how often do you see the leader of the organization? If they are line managed, how often do you see their line manager?

If you are the leader of a large children's centre or a multi-number of centres that operates across a number of different locations you may consider gaining feedback from different groups of staff in relation to their perception of your visibility or remoteness. How much time are you able to spend in each location? Larger and complex organizations demand the use of different leadership styles than smaller more compact ones. One big issue here is that organizations set up structures to lead and manage the people who work within them, and this can lead directly to a shift for the leaders away from the core activities of the organization and away from the day-to-day contact with the majority of the staff.

Reflective task

Think carefully about the organization in which you work and the distance between the leader and the rest of the organization. Consider the reasons and the specific job roles that make this the case? Are there things that the leader can do to change this situation?

Choose to lead

To begin this section we would like you to start with a reflective task about your view of leadership posts.

Reflective task

If you are already a leader consider how you got to this position. Did you make a conscious decision to apply for a leadership post? Did you take on the post on a temporary basis and end up taking it on full time? What did you think you had to offer the post and the organization? What difference did you think you it might make?

If you are not a leader yet, what attracts you to being a leader? Is it the thought of being in charge? Have you seen others in a leadership role and thought that you could do things better or differently? You may find it helpful to go back to your notes for the activities in Chapter 1 in which you reviewed your experiences of being led to help you with this task.

Be the person others choose to follow

Leaders recognize the need to attract followers. 'Followership' has recently been studied as a key to understanding leadership. To follow, people must feel confidence in the direction in which the leader is headed. They are enabled and empowered to do their part in accomplishing the stated objectives. Followers need to believe that, at the end of the journey, they will be recognized and rewarded for their contribution. The leader must help followers answer the question, 'What's in it for me?' Successful leaders are honest about the potential risks inherent in the chosen path. They communicate not just the overall direction but any information followers need to successfully and skilfully carry out their responsibilities.

Kelley (1992) constructed a topology for five types of followers in organizations.

Alienated followers. Alienated followers are deep and independent thinkers who do not willingly commit to any leader.

Passive followers. Passive followers do as they are told but do not think critically and are not particularly active participants.

Conformist followers. Conformists are more participative than passive followers, but do not provide a particular challenge.

Pragmatic followers. Pragmatic followers are middling in their independence, engagement and general contribution.

Exemplary followers. Exemplary followers are ideal in almost all ways, excelling at all tasks, engaging strongly with the group and providing intelligent yet sensitive support and challenge to the leader.

Provide vision for the future

Leaders have a clear vision for the organization. They share a dream and direction that other people want to share and follow. The leadership vision goes beyond any written organizational mission statement and your vision statement and ideally will be constructed with others so they have ownership of the ideas that go to make up the final vision for the organization. The vision of leadership permeates the workplace and is manifested in the actions, beliefs, values and goals of your leadership role.

Reflective task

Existing leaders

Have you a set of values and a vision for the organization in which you work? Have other members of staff had any input to the vision? Have you shared and discussed the vision?

Aspiring leaders

How might you begin to share your vision for services for children and their families? Do you have a clear idea of what your values are?

Demonstrate genuine concern for others

A key finding from the work of Beverley Alimo-Metcalf and John Alban Metcalf (2003) on transformational leaders is that the single most important impact factor in the effectiveness of leaders is the genuine concern for others. She sees leadership as about having the ability to create relationships and good working environments rather than merely possessing competencies.

Scales measured by the transformational leadership questionnaire (TLQ)

Leading and developing others (1)

Showing genuine concern

Genuine interest in staff as individuals; values their contributions; develops their strengths; coaches, mentors; has positive expectations of what his/her staff can achieve

Empowering: Trusts staff to take decisions/initiatives on important matters; delegates effectively; develops staff's potential

Being accessible: Approachable and not status conscious; prefers face-to-face communication; accessible and keeps in touch

Encouraging change: Encourages questioning of traditional approaches to the job; encourages new approaches/solutions to problems; encourages strategic thinking

Personal qualities (2)

Being transparent: Honest and consistent in behaviour; more concerned with the good of the organization than personal ambition

Acting with integrity: Open to criticism and disagreement; consults and involves others in decision making; regards values as integral to the organization

Being decisive: Decisive when required; prepared to take difficult decisions, and risks when appropriate

Inspiring others: Charismatic; exceptional communicator, inspires others to join him/her

Resolving complex problems: Capacity to deal with a wide range of complex issues; creative in problem solving

Leading the organization

Networking and achieving: Inspiring communication of the vision of the organization/service to a wide network of internal and external stakeholders; gains the confidence and support of various groups through sensitivity to needs, and by achieving organization goals

Focusing team effort: Clarifies objectives and boundaries; team oriented to problem solving and decision making, and to identifying values

Building shared vision: Has a clear vision and strategic direction, which she/he engages various internal and external stakeholders in developing; draws others together in achieving the vision

Supporting a developmental culture: Supportive when mistakes are made; encourages critical feedback of him/herself and the service provided

Facilitating change sensitively: Sensitivity to the impact of change on different parts of the organization; maintains a balance between change and stability

Reflective task

Think about the items identified in the TLQ and then look back at the standards for your role or the role to which you aspire. What are the key differences and similarities between the lists? Which standards focus on showing a genuine concern for others or is this element missing with the list focusing on competencies alone?

Designing a metaphor for your leadership development

Metaphor as we saw in Chapter 3 can be helpful in identifying the differences between two conceptual areas in this case: management and leadership. Metaphors are powerful shortcuts to instant and memorable understanding. They evoke vivid images and allow us to 'see' things from a new perspective, and so are useful tools for creative development. In this case they can also be helpful for creating our own images of concepts that we wish to develop further. For example White and Prywes (2007) focus on the differences in leadership styles between reptiles and mammals as a metaphor for their associated approaches.

Habits of the mind of the cold and warm blooded leaders

Reptiles	Mammals
Detached	Engaged
Analytical	Emotional
Quantitative	Qualitative
Independent	Interdependent
Adversarial	Cooperative
Focus on control	Emphasis on freedoms
Faith in evidence	Faith in others
Rely on audits	Rely on trust
Values contracts	Value community

Source: White, and Prywes (2007: 27–8)

We take this idea and develop this further not looking at comparisons but the leadership role as a whole in this next section.

Metaphor	Examples
Gardener	The leader is the gardener tending the plants in the garden applying nutrients when needed, supporting against frosts, looking out for weeds, etc.
Sports team coach	Selecting the team, setting up the training, coaching the team to its best performance, nursing any injuries, thinking up the game plan
Parent	Feeding, clothing, supporting and caring, teaching and training towards independence
'The fat controller'	If you are not familiar with Thomas the Tank engine this initial might not make much sense but the idea is you are responsible for the smooth running of the railway, its engines and all the coaches, wagons and the line guiding but also allowing for expertise in specific areas
Orchestra conductor	This leader has the full score with everyone's part included, they bring in the soloists and their expertise at the correct point in the music, they keep everyone in time and the music sounds good when they do so
Belayer in rock climbing	The big idea is that the climber is on one end of the rope and the belayer is on the other end. If the climber falls, the belayer is the person that keeps the climber from hitting the ground. This doesn't feel like a very glamorous job as the belayer doesn't get the glory of getting to the top of a mountain first but they support others to get there for the team.

Reflective task

After reading these suggested metaphors for good leaders what kind of a metaphor would help you to develop your leadership further? You might find it helpful to draw pictures of your ideas and to share these with others.

Might there be any difficulties associated with establishing a metaphor?

Thinking through your personal approach to leadership development

Developmental opportunity	Examples	Advantages	Disadvantages
Specifically tailored and non-accredited leadership development programmes – open access.	Programmes, run by the National School of Government, NCSL [National College for School Leadership].	Brings together specific learning communities – often from a range of sectors and settings. When residential there is a stronger learning community potential.	Generally high cost. Time away from work – they can cover ground not relevant to the personal setting and can work to a core curriculum that does reflect personal learning needs.
Short in house leadership programmes .	Where training and management development consultancies are commissioned to deliver programmes aimed at building internal organizational capacity.	Can be highly cost-effective. Creates the opportunity to tailor content to personal, group and organizational needs. Often run by people with a deep understanding of the contextual setting. Can focus on the delivery of organizational objectives and needs.	May focus on the needs of the organization more than the needs of the individual. Learning affected by internal and interpersonal politics between attendees. May at times be based on notions of leadership that are inappropriate to the setting. Examples of consultants selling their wares and ideas to closed communities.
External accredited programmes. These often have specific eligibility criteria to meet before places are available on these programmes.	Programmes run by large institutional bodies such as Universities – offering accreditation at a variety of levels or NCSL programmes like NPQICL or NPQH [National Professional Qualification for Headship].	Can be based on sound theory. Attaining qualifications can be a significant motivational driver for participants and can bring career opportunities. Often have sound learning communities and opportunities to participate in alumni activities.	May lack behavioural elements of leadership and focus on pedagogic notions of learning. Can be relatively expensive.

(Continued)

Developmental opportunity	Examples	Advantages	Disadvantages
Personal one-to-one coaching activities.	Individual leaders working to a highly tailored and specific agenda around personal development with an external, experienced coach.	The learning becomes very personal and behaviourally anchored in the needs of the personal and the setting. The learning agenda can be focused on the needs of the individual and not the organization. Can be highly cost-effective and of minimum disruption to the job.	While it can be cost-effective, certain professional coaches don't come cheap. May stray into areas that become hard to deal with. A lot of personal coaches are lacking even a basic theoretical understanding of the learning and coaching process. Careful thought needs to be applied when searching for the appropriate coach.
Signing up for participating in 360 multi-rater feedback exercises.	Participating in seeking feedback from staff, peers, bosses and others in a structured and mechanistic feedback process involving a report and reference to baseline and group norms.	Can be highly cost-effective and massively developmental when handled ethically. Can be a very cost-effective form of personal development when coupled to expert facilitation and the subsequent establishment of a personal development plan.	Some extremely questionable instruments on the market. In certain organizational settings the output of 360 instruments are handled with little finesse and there are too many examples on unethical administration of 360 – especially when people are cast adrift and have no personal, confidential facilitation support.
Shadowing.	A valued and experienced leader is sought to open up their world to an aspirant leader or an individual who is keen to extend their personal leadership.	Can be cost-effective. Can have significant personal benefits if the right person to shadow is chosen and a clear and unambiguous contract is established at the outset.	Can be reduced to just a bit of fun looking at someone else at work. Can be highly unpredictable in outcome – especially if there is no clear contract at the outset. Difficult to choose the right person. May need to be coupled to engagement with another person to act as mentor to allow for reflective learning to take place.
Mentoring.	A one on one learning and reflective relationship.	When the right mentor is chosen can be one of the most profound and effective forms of leadership development. Remarkable to note that many individuals who enjoy high leadership reputations report having a mentor. Works best when there is a clear contract and escape mechanism for both parties in the event of failure.	For some, when it goes wrong it can be difficult for either party to escape from. May lead the mentee down the garden path. Can dissolve into a relationship that is anything but mentoring.

(Continued)

Developmental opportunity	Examples	Advantages	Disadvantages
Participating in action learning sets.	Action-learning sets – as groups of individual with similar agenda and contracted bond of trust brought together in a systematic form of reflective learning – often with an experienced facilitator.	Manageable time commitment and generally cost-effective. When action-learning sets work well they can produce learning opportunities with the most impact we can engage with. Expert facilitators can make action-learning sets highly relevant to both the institutional setting and the needs of individuals. Another learning and development methodology that requires a clear and unambiguous contract and set of agreed rules to work well – when they are in place action-learning sets can have a long and productive life.	It is a methodology that does not suit everyone. Some learning set activity can verge on the therapeutic and set participants may find this highly challenging and not meeting their learning preferences. Some set facilitators should not be let anywhere near professionals in challenging jobs.
Personalized and individually structured personal research.	Setting one's own leadership development plan.	Cost and time effective. Can reap huge motivational rewards especially for those who have a strong individualized and personal learning preference.	We can lead ourselves up the garden path! Can be poor at translating theory into practice unless coupled to another learning and development methodology.

Where does 360 fit into leadership development?

Many leadership development exercises are built around 360 instruments. In recent years there has been criticism of many 360 instruments especially where they have been applied to circumstances that are less than ethical.

The background to 360 multi-rater feedback instruments is a case study in its own right but more and more existing and aspiration leaders are being offered participation in 360 appraisal systems. Appraisal is a vital aspect of obtaining performance feedback in work settings and by and large it is for many a very positive process. It does however have a number of weaknesses. Not least of which is the bias that bosses can place on the system. Quite simply what I as an individual leader wish to place emphasis on the job may be different from what my boss may wish to place an emphasis upon. Establishing who is right can therefore become a very difficult issue to resolve. As we know when looking at leadership in hierarchies we place very different emphasis upon our personal leadership preferences of those that are distant to us as opposed to those who are close, or nearby us. Shamir (1995) in his research drew some very important distinctions in this in his research. He pointed out that we might expect distant leaders – those with whom we have little or even no formal social interaction with – to have certain characteristics that are very different from those we are close to.

In large complex organizational settings I as an individual may expect the distant corporate leader to have say characteristics of great presence, gifted powers of oratory and be 'charismatic'. But, if my nearby leader, the person I report directly to had these dominant characteristics as a leader I may feel very different about that person. I might expect my nearby leader to have a real and genuine concern for me, understand in depth the context in which I work and have sympathy and understanding for the detail of my day-to-day work challenges. Therefore in appraisal situations we can see how easy it is to fall into the trap of negotiating targets and objectives and even service outcomes that are more in accord with the bosses aspiration than our own. Whoever is right is to miss the point, it is the fact that there is this inbuilt bias in the system that makes appraisal a very hit and miss affair for many.

Out of this concern grew a technology of averaging the ratings around a set of pre-agreed criterion which represents performance in the job that matches a self-rating with the average of the boss, chosen peers and key direct reports. Some systems in commercial settings even include customers and clients in the process, and indeed in public sector organizations it is not uncommon to have categories for others. Senior leaders in local authorities for instance often seek feedback from elected members.

To make this system work well though there need to be a number of pre-agreed criteria in the process. The obvious question to ask is how confidential is the process? Most people do not feel comfortable in knowing exactly how they have been rated by others, indeed publishing all the ratings of others is a certain way of distorting a 360 report. If I as an individual am called upon to rate my boss and he or she is going to know that I have rated them low on a key aspect of their approach to leadership it might have some very career limiting outcomes. But, if my rating is to be anonymized and obscured by averaging all the bosses' ratings then I am likely to be fair and honest in my response. In fact this overall non-attributive response is more developmental and useful than knowing exactly how I have been rated alongside others. This will be explained in more detail a little later in this chapter.

Before we go any further we do need to draw a distinction between the differing types of 360 there are on the market. A quick trawl of the web will result in vast numbers of consultants and instrument publishers leading to arguments as to why their product is better than others but we need to take care here. There are instruments on the market that are built around transferable models of management, the questions they contain are about the functional skills that many in managerial positions undertake, irrespective of setting or sector. For instance most managers chair meetings so there will be questions such as:

'The manager I am rating chairs meetings effectively.'

There will then usually be a rating scale something like 1 = Is highly ineffective to 6 = Is highly skilled at chairing meetings.

Such instruments have a place but the content is not what we would call 'behaviourally anchored', in other words it is simply a pure statement of a kind of managerial competence and the overall response may tell us little about how well this person chairs meetings in a variety of contexts.

The second type of instrument is one that is behaviourally anchored and generally has well-researched and valid questions in their content. By valid we mean they have content validity, the questions they ask are soundly rooted in the context that the person being rated operates. It is these latter instruments that we are concerned with in leadership development. It is also the root cause of many of the concerns that are now evident about the misuse of 360 instruments. It is not unknown for organizations to try to extract something from 360 reports that does not exist, and although we see a rightful place for appropriate 360 instruments in leadership development we feel examples of misuse are now all too common.

A key issue with 360 reports is that you may get an overall score that leads you as the recipient to believe that as all the people you have asked to rate you on a particular element of your leadership rate you lower than you rate yourself does not always mean that you have a clear development need in this area. Just because up to ten or so people appear to agree with something it does not mean they are right and you are wrong. There is of course a clear opportunity for bias in the system, there are stories of managers discovering that all the people invited to rate them have a had a meeting and plotted to score them low just to get one over on them, but thankfully this is not common and is indeed quite impractical if the system has been set up correctly. This is where we come to the true output of a 360 report, we need to see it as a hypothesis that needs to be tested and not as an empirical set of data that is an absolute predictor of your performance.

Application of 360 in the early years

On some leadership programmes elements of a 360 approach are built in to the overall design. On NPQICL there is an oral approach to this technique for the final centre assessment visit in which the assessor talks to people that the participant works for, with and those who work for the participant. This gives an opportunity for the participant to gain feedback from a range of people and the assessor to see the participant's leadership in relation to different groups of staff. There can be clear differences between groups of people in relation to how they see someone's leadership skills. Sometimes these can be explained by the person's knowledge or proximity to the leader, which means they may be basing their perceptions on more limited knowledge. Sometimes it can be that the leader has strengths in communicating well with the community but not so well to their line manager. The process does give a more rounded view of the participant.

Reflective task

Can you think of ways you might be able to get feedback about leadership from people who experience your leadership from different perspectives, for example your line manager, your staff, colleagues, parents and even children?

Summary of key ideas in this chapter

- Metaphors can be helpful in identifying the specific component parts of the role of leader.
- There are advantages and disadvantages to different forms of continuing professional development for your leadership.
- 360 instruments can be helpful in feedback about different people's perception of you in a leadership role and can be used then to target areas of development.

Further reading

Alimo-Metcalf, B. and Alban Metcalf, J. (2003). Leadership in Public Sector Organizations, in Storey (ed.) *Leadership Organizations: Current Issues and Key Trends*. London: Routledge

Kelley, R. (1992). *The Power of Followership*. New York: Bantam Dell

Useful websites

http://www.ncsl.org.uk/

http://www.surestart.gov.uk/

http://www.teachernet.gov.uk

http://www.scie.org.uk/

http://www.kingsfund.org.uk/leadership/index.html

All the above websites were last accessed on 21.09.08.

8 Developing Leadership in Others and the Organizations

Chapter Outline

Working with others and developing their leadership

One of the hardest challenges for leaders is working with others and developing their leadership. This is sometimes seen as succession planning (Hirsh 2000) in which you are identifying people within the organization to take on roles of responsibility later in their careers. However, here it is more than that although succession planning is part of the process. There may be people working with you who do not aspire to become a leader in relation to a specific role but would welcome the opportunity to take on a role in developing specific areas of interest within the organization and championing this area throughout their work. It can give people a taste of what leadership can be like so they can make appropriate decisions about their own career paths but above all it opens up ownership of work of the organization allowing others to take decisions. It would appear that in most early years settings with the breadth of expectation, outputs and outcomes required that highly distributed forms of leadership are highly appropriate to the purpose and structure of such organizations. The early years leader must in these terms invest energy, commitment and time to ensuring that leadership talent is encouraged in others, irrespective of their position or role.

Standards that this chapter will help you explore are:

Early Years: S33, S34, S35, S36

Social Care: Functional area A, Functional area B, Functional area C, Functional area D, Functional area E and Functional area F

Children's centre leaders: 1. Leading learning and development, 2. Stronger families, stronger communities, 3. Being accountable and responsible, 4. Shaping the present and creating the future, 5. Managing the organization, 6. Building and strengthening teams

Teaching: Q5, Q6, Q32, Q33, C5, C6, C40, C41, P9, P10, E13, E14, E15, A2, A3, Shaping the future, Leading learning and teaching, Developing self and working with others, Managing the organization, Securing accountability, Strengthening community

By the end of this chapter you will:

- have explored how leaders impact upon the culture of the organization and develop a learning organization
- have explored the relationship between leaders and followers
- have explored the differences between delegation and developing leadership in others

How leaders impact upon and develop organization cultures and value systems (climates)

When we look at leaders in early years settings we can see that a significant challenge is to ensure that certain values and practices get a 'grip' within the organization. Lets for a moment think about this notion of grip. We can see that many organizations in many different settings have a kind of life that is sustained even when people change. Many large corporations have become household names and survive for long periods of time with consistent values, products and image. This is an interesting phenomena, but it does present a challenge for leaders in early years settings. There are many settings that have long standing traditions, especially those that have grown out of localized nurseries in communities, but it would be fair to say that many are new institutions with a new clarity of purpose that is driven by a mixture of social and educational policy and need. But how many years will it take before they can be traditional institutions in localities such as many schools are? It is the role of the leader to create the core 'life' that is often referred to as organizational culture. The argument here is that if leadership were to be one side of the coin then culture would be the other. The depth of interdependence between the two concepts cannot be underestimated. Some of the most effective leaders are those that know they are playing a significant part in building a sustainable and supportive culture within their organization. There is however a cautionary note to be made here. We must draw a clear distinction between those leaders who are out to build an organization around the cult of the person or their personality. Too often have we seen powerful leaders that build cultures around fear and coercion, they dominate to such an extent they are only happy if they have sycophantic and obedient followership, they are often less than happy places to be, either as a service user or as an employee. What we are arguing for here is a form of leadership that impacts upon culture that transmits a sense of collective leadership that is not wholly dependent upon one person in the leadership population.

This of course has a major impact upon our thinking around recruitment and selection. Do, or should leaders when they are looking to recruit others into leadership positions or positions with leadership potential seek out others who hold similar values to themselves? Early years leaders clearly need to recruit and develop others who 'fit' into the broader needs and requirements of the organization culture and values systems, but the most effective leaders know that this is dynamic and where challenge, debate and discussion around the appropriateness of the culture to the organizations purpose are transparent these create the most healthy organizational cultures. To do this, it is therefore vital to work tirelessly to encourage and bring out leadership in others. An organizational culture that has the capacity to distribute leadership, develops leadership capacity in others irrespective of how they are placed in the organization is likely to have a sustainable future.

One, perhaps apocryphal story to illustrate the importance of culture and how powerful it is comes from zoology. Researchers were studying dominance in a troop of primates in a zoo. They had noticed that there was a strong preference for the most dominant to take the freshest fruit from the top of tree in the enclosure. The least preferred source of fruit was that which had fallen to the ground. The researchers placed high velocity cold-water jets in the top of the tree and when the primates went to collect the fruit they were faced with a very uncomfortable jet of water. They would leave the fruit and dash down the tree making a great deal of noise. What the researchers then did was to remove a small number of the most dominant primates and introduce new less dominant members to the troop. Eventually fewer and fewer primates were left who had actually experienced the blast of cold water when they climbed to the top of the tree and after a period of time with removing small numbers of primates and introducing new ones to the troop there was a profound behaviour change in the troop. No primate had climbed to the top of the tree, not one had ever even tried and not one sought to take the most desirable food from the top of the tree any more. A new corporate memory had been introduced to the troop without there being any primate in the troop who actually had any experience of the discomfort of feeling a blast of cold water when approaching the most desirable source of food.

While we have tried but sadly we cannot verify this tale but it does however underscore how powerful leadership and culture can be. It is also a cautionary note for leaders who can inadvertently reinforce potentially negative aspects of working in the organization, even if they have the best of intentions.

Reflective task

Think back to when you started a new job and try and recall what the 'induction' process contained for you?

Then think about what you really learned about that place a few months later.

Usually you receive some information on fire drills, have a chat with HR about holiday arrangement and quickly you obtain the basic information you need to function in the role you have taken on. There are, however, in most organizations the rules that are never written down, these often come in the form of stories. Some organizations and settings have some mythologies that have a huge grip on the organization. An incident at a leaving party, an individual's behaviour at a meeting – it can be almost anything. But the stories that build around these incidents are vital in building the 'reality' that the early settings will have leaders play a crucial role through being both careful and respectful of these stories and mythologies as they can be forces for both good and bad.

How then can we develop appropriate attitudes to the culture of the organization in those who will be leading specific parts of the organization or projects or becoming the leaders of the organization in the future? One area is by raising the awareness in others about the importance culture plays in the organization. Therefore we feel that the most effective leaders are the ones who carefully manage the opportunities to raise debate and discussion around the value system and culture within the setting. This needs to be completed in a very sensitive way but by its very definition the process can dictate the culture.

What can we take from early years practice?

Many of you may come from an early years professional background and are therefore used to working directly with children guiding them in their learning during the day. You may be stimulating their curiosity, negotiating, encouraging and facilitating to mention just a few skills. Rodd (2006) when talking about effective leaders in early childhood mentions that 'they are interested in empowering, restructuring, teaching and acting as role models, encouraging openness and stimulating questioning.' These are just the skills that you would be using as a good early years practitioner and although you might consider these appropriate with children you may not immediately see the relevance of using the same skills in working with adults. This is different from pedagogical leadership though you are leading the learning within the organization for all learners both children and adults.

Reflective task

Even if you are not an early years practitioner there are skills that you use as part of your professional role that you transfer to working with adults in a team situation. Think about what those might be.

Establishing trust and teamwork

There are many types of teams. What follows is not a complete range of teams as there are other typologies or classifications that could be considered. We have chosen a few, which we think directly, relate to activities in the early years.

Service and production teams – examples are in production, construction, sales and health care. They have a relatively long life-span, providing an ongoing product or service to customers or the organization. In early years settings these might be around teaching teams, teams around the child or family.

Project and development teams – including research and product development teams. They are dedicated to a particular objective, and have limited life-spans and a clear set of short-term objectives. They are often cross-functional, with members selected for the contribution their expertise can make. Advisory boards for the initial set up of children's centres might be an example of this in the early years though their specific function will alter as the project develops from set up to implementation. Another example might be a group brought together to explore different ways of providing focused support for children in a setting. Research could be carried out to look at a range of models for intervention and the team might include different professionals.

Involvement teams – with the aim of improving, for example improving the quality of the provision of a specific activity or the involvement of parents. Members will not devote a great deal of time to them, and once they have achieved their objectives they should be disbanded. The ideas here are that they have a focused goal and that the achievement of the goal means that the team is no longer needed.

Virtual teams – who work in separate buildings and who may even be in different countries. Such teams may also fit into one of the above categories, such as project and development. They may need to communicate by telephone, email and teleconferencing rather than face-to-face. Managing them is particularly difficult, not least because remote working can exacerbate misunderstandings. This is a specific example of how teams might be configured across several settings for example children's centres and satellite locations.

Benefits of team working

Early years organizations that have introduced team working suggest that the benefits are as follows:

to improve quality of services for children and their families
to speed the sharing of ideas across the organization
to respond to opportunities and threats and to fast-changing environments of children's services
to increase staff motivation
to introduce multi-skilling and staff flexibility

There can be benefits for staff too suggesting that people have greater job satisfaction and motivation, and improved opportunities for learning associated with work. Team working does not happen instantly because you bring people together and it needs skilful management and resources devoted to it, or initiatives may fail.

The main stages of teamwork adapted from the original work of Tuckman (1965) are as follows:

- **Forming** – or undeveloped, when people are working as individuals rather than a team.
- **Storming** – teams need to pass through a stage of conflict if they are to achieve their potential. The team becomes more aggressive, internally and in relation to outside groups, rules and requirements.
- **Norming** – or consolidating, in which the team is beginning to achieve its potential, effectively applying the resource it has to the tasks it has, using a process it has developed by itself.
- **Performing** – when the team is characterized by openness and flexibility. It challenges itself constantly but without emotionally charged conflict, and places a high priority on the development of other team members.
- **Mourning** – when the team disbands.

Reflective task

Think about teams/groups that you have been a member of and consider how the stages outlined match your experiences. What were the most difficult parts of being a member of the team/group? Can you think about what happened to make the work within the team/group easier? How will this influence the way you might form and work with teams/groups as a leader in the early years?

Trust

Trust is essential if effective teamwork is to take place and at each of the stages outlined above. When there is trust in a team it is possible to challenge ideas and preconceived notions in order to develop the thinking of the group. It can though be easy for teams to develop ways of working that is within their 'comfort zone' and on the surface the work of the team appears to be effective. However, in order to develop, further 'disequilibration' (Piaget 1977) in the group can create new ways of thinking. The important issue is that people do not feel that the challenge is a personal one, and it is designed to promote discussion and development. In a trusting team it is possible to explore the reasons why challenge may be useful. If linked with ideas about members of the team taking 'guardianship' of specific areas of the services then all members of the team can provide appropriate levels of challenge associated with their chosen areas to guard. In contrast Ringer (2002) says that when anxiety is raised past that which is tolerable, groups' members retreat, which limits the group's connectivity. For the leader, the balancing act is to provide the right amount of challenge while not raising the anxiety levels so that people withdraw from the group and are therefore not engaging with any discussions or activities.

Challenges can come from a variety of sources. A new member of the team can upset the balance of the working relationships as the existing team and the new member get to know each other. For the leader this can feel as those they are going backwards. Time spent at this point revisiting the ground rules for the team can be helpful in inducting the new person into the group but also to remind the rest of the group how and why the team operates as it does. Are there any changes that need to be made not just to accommodate the new person but to acknowledge the development of the team as a working group?

Establish an environment for continuous improvement

This sounds a really good idea but it is more difficult to establish than first appears. The initial reaction of many people asked to think about continually reviewing practice is that a leader is looking for someone to blame rather than developing reflective practice where looking at what has gone well and what could be improved is a part of the practice in the setting. The notions of reflective practice come from Schön (1983) with the following key ideas:

'Reflective Practicum'

This is Schön's term for the educational setting, or environment: 'A practicum is a setting designed for the task of learning a practice.' (1987: 37). This is where students learn *by doing*, with the help of coaching. He tells us the practicum is 'reflective' in two senses: 'it is intended to help students become proficient in a kind of reflection-in-action; and, when it works well, it involves a dialogue of coach and student that takes the form of reciprocal reflection-in-action' (1987: 37). In early years settings the students become the children in the settings.

Tacit knowledge

He describes for example the remarkable way we are able to pick out a familiar face in a crowd. This does not require thinking about, or a systematic analysis of features. We cannot verbalize how this is done, and so the knowledge is 'unspoken' or 'tacit'. In early years settings seeing a skilled practitioner at work much of what they do becomes intuitive.

Knowing-in-action

This idea derives from the idea of tacit knowledge. It refers to the kinds of knowledge we can only reveal in the way we carry out tasks and approach problems. 'The knowing is *in* the action. It is revealed by the skilful execution of the performance – we are characteristically unable to make it verbally explicit' Schön (1983: 51). This tacit knowledge is derived from research, and also from the practitioner's own reflections and experience.

Reflection-in-action

This is the kind of reflection that occurs while a problem is being addressed, in what Schön calls the 'action-present'. It is a response to a surprise – where the expected outcome is outside of our knowing-in-action. The reflective process is at least to some degree conscious, but may not be verbalized. Reflection-in-action is about challenging our assumptions (because knowing-in-action forms the basis of assumption). It is about thinking again, in a new way, about a problem we have encountered.

Reflection-on-action

This is reflection after the event, it is consciously undertaken, and often documented. This can be seen as part of any evaluation process by a practitioner as well as with feedback from others such as participants.

Willing suspension of disbelief

This term describes the process of entering into an experience, without judgement, in order to learn from it. Schön uses the term in relation to the idea of learning by doing. We cannot will ourselves to 'believe' until one understands though understanding often will only arise from experience. So it is necessary first to allow the experience to happen.

Operative attention

This is listening and absorbing information, in a state of readiness to apply and experiment with the new information. An example in an early years setting would be when we listen to directions on how to complete a complex task. This participation is important in the learning process – a learner needs to be already engaged in activity for further information to have meaning. The mechanical or imperfect performance of an activity prepares the learner for new information (feedback) on that activity, in order to develop understanding.

The ladder of reflection

Schön talks about a vertical dimension of analysis that can happen in the dialogue between learner and teacher. To move up a rung on the ladder involves reflecting on an activity. To move down a rung is to move from reflection to experimentation. This ladder has more than two rungs and it is also possible to reflect on the process of reflection. The importance of this concept is in its potential for helping out with 'stuck' situations in learning. The action of being able to move to another level may assist coach and learner to achieve together what Schön refers to as 'convergence of meaning'.

Reflective task

Think about how you might use these ideas to get colleagues to reflect upon their activities both with children if directly involved with them and in working with adults as their learners? Do you use any of these ideas yourself that you could share with the team?

Establish organizational learning

Ideas about organizational learning have been part of management literature for many years, but they have become more widespread since the 1990s. Part of the reason why these ideas have become more prominent is the focus by academics looking at organizational learning and a number of consultancies have seen this as an area of potential development in their work with organizations. In many ways it builds upon the ideas of reflective practice from Schön (1983) and translates that from the individual across the whole organization. The advantages of this approach are that the people working in the organization are learning together and share a common vision of how the organization could develop. Together they become a 'community of practice' combining the work of Schön (1983) and Wenger (1998).

Easterby-Smith, Burgoyne and Araujo (1999: 3–5):

> The *technical* view assumes that organizational learning is about the effective processing, interpretation of, and response to, information both inside and outside the organization. This information may be quantitative or qualitative, but is generally explicit and in the public domain . . .. The *social perspective* on organization learning focuses on the way people make sense of their experiences at work. These experiences may derive from explicit sources such as financial information, or they may be derived from tacit sources, such as the 'feel' that a skilled craftsperson has, or the intuition possessed by a skilled strategist. From this view, learning is something that can emerge from social interactions, normally in the natural work setting. In the case of explicit information it involves a joint process of making sense of data . . . The more tacit and 'embodied' forms of learning involve situated practices, observation and emulation of skilled practitioners and socialization into a community of practice.

Provide opportunities for people to grow both personally and professionally

One difficult area in organizations is that the organization itself has an action plan, development plan or other means of identifying the direction of its development. Sometimes personal development needs may not fit exactly with the development needs of the organization. It is important that any target setting approach whether that be through supervision, one to ones of appraisal results in a balance of targets providing opportunities for both personal and organizational development. In some multi-agency teams an individual's professional development may need to be outside the organization. An example of this might be a social worker who is employed by a school or children's centre who will need access to the continual professional development associated with social work as well as professional and personal development opportunities within the organization.

Sharing management duties

This can include practical activities such as the sharing of chairing of meeting duties and/or taking down the minutes so that the skills are learnt and practised by all members of the team. Learning how to do rotas and the difficulties associated with meeting everyone's needs can be a learning experience. This can appear to be delegating tasks in as part of being a manager yet if discussed beforehand can be seen as leaders taking on a 'followership' role and allowing others to take a lead in a whole range of tasks within the organization.

Mentoring

Mentoring is described as 'help by one person to another in making significant transitions in knowledge, work or thinking' Clutterbuck and Megginson (1999: 8).

Mentoring can be helpful in developing leadership in others as it can be used to explore one person's ideas using the other as a non-judgemental sounding board. The first person observes, listens and asks questions to be able to fully understand the situation being described. Depending upon the type of mentoring they may offer suggestions of things for the mentee to think about, but this is entirely up to the mentee. It can be established with pairs of people within an organization as long as the boundaries are clearly defined and information discussed in mentoring sessions is not used anywhere else unless the mentee chooses to do so. Sometimes people feel more comfortable talking to a mentor who though might have some experience of the professional contact outside the organization so the two things work and mentoring sessions are kept completely separate. The following table explores in more detail some of the issues in relation to mentoring and how two different approaches can work for the same issues.

Issue	Traditional mentor led approach	Tailored participant led approach
1 It is hard to find a mentor.	Finding a good mentor can be very hard, Many people have a mentor that is agreed for them by other stakeholders in the process and the outcomes can be at best variable. Many people can therefore stick with a mentor who is not either appropriate or can mislead the participant.	While recognizing that finding the best mentor can be difficult within the tailored approach there is more emphasis placed upon the participant driving the process even if there are guidelines to follow and special career or professional imperatives to be met.

(Continued)

	Issue	Traditional mentor led approach	Tailored participant led approach
2	The mentor does not appear to be addressing the issues I need for my development.	Where the starting point is the development of a pool of mentors, even with careful and structured mentor training there is more power on the shoulders of the mentor rather than the person being mentored and this can and often does result in drift in the process.	Control is in the hands of the person being mentored. Issues are brought to the mentor in a structured way and the participant is in control of the content of the interchanges between the mentor and themselves.
3	Do I choose an 'in house' or external mentor?	Little choice is often offered where the mentor is in control of the process. Escaping an internal mentor can be almost impossible for many.	For the participant the choice is much easier, if an internal mentor is identified then as long as they meet the specification that is OK. Different contracting still needs to take place with an internal mentor but the participant is still more in control.
4	How do I avoid drift in the process?	Very difficult if the mentor is doing the participant a favour.	The escape clause is enacted with the control being in the hands of the participant.
5	The relationship is more directive than reflective.	Participants are reluctant to go back to the pool afraid of how this may look to programme managers.	The participant considers style as part of their personal mentor specification. If the mentor does not keep to the style and approach required the participant can evoke the escape clause. The failure is now in the hands of the participant who may not have either specified correctly or they may have misunderstood their requirements.
6	Mentor does not address the key strategic issues facing the profession or sector.	Often covered up in the process. In many cases mentors can detract from the strategic target by having an approach which is about overt support for them but covert opposition to change.	As reputations are often built upon what people openly say and not on what they actually feel about the strategic change issues the initial contracting phase is made more robust in the participant led approach to mentoring and is there more likely to be exposed at an early stage and the participant may not find themselves in a relationship that does not deliver the strategic imperatives required.

Coaching

Coaching is

> a process that enables learning and development to occur and thus performance to improve. To be a successful a Coach requires a knowledge and understanding of process as well as the variety of styles, skills and techniques that are appropriate to the context in which the coaching takes place. Parsloe (1999: 8)

There are similarities between the two but the main difference is that mentoring, particularly in its traditional sense, enables an individual to follow in the path of an older and wiser colleague who can pass on knowledge, experience and open doors to otherwise out-of-reach opportunities. Coaching on the other hand is not generally performed on the basis that the coach has direct experience of their participant's formal occupational role unless the coaching is specific and skills focused.

Both mentoring and coaching may focus on one or more of the following areas:

Business
Executive
Performance
Skills
Personal

Linking with other organizations to share experiences and expertise

One way of developing leadership in others is to enable them to see different models of leadership in action. This can be achieved by visiting and shadowing other leaders in different organizations. Leadership is also possible across organizations when people are brought together to work on specific projects.

> A group of people working on a common project do not necessarily invoke the group process. If the group is managed in a totally autocratic manner, there may be little opportunity for interaction relating to the work. (Blair 1991)

Projects across organizations can provide opportunities to allow for leadership to be developed in a number of staff. It is important that when working with other professionals that you consider the ethics involved and the following guidance from the National Association of Social Workers for an American site (1999) Social Workers Ethical Responsibilities to colleagues Section 2 is helpful to start your thinking about how you might operate in such groups and how you might guide others to begin their leadership with cross-professional groups.

> . . . 'avoid unwarranted negative criticism of colleagues with clients or other professional.
>
> . . . comments that refer to level of competence.
>
> . . . cooperate with colleague of other professional when such cooperation serves the well being of clients.' (1999)

Work–life balance

There is a need to make leadership posts attractive to other members of staff in order that there are people to take on the leadership roles in the future. One difficulty is the work–life balance that people see that the leader has or hasn't got in their current leadership role. It can appear to others that by taking on a leadership position that the leader gives up on their balance of work and other life activities. If leaders are seen to take on work over and above the post then it can appear that leaders have no work–life balance and the role ceases to look attractive to others. Leadership roles need to be attractive and feasible for others to take on the role or even consider it.

Distributed leadership

In the existing literature this is a difficult area to clearly define as it is linked to the different definitions of leadership. As we have seen earlier in this book the definition of leadership is continuing to change and develop. Gronn's (2002) work focuses on two main notions of distributed leadership; first that of numerical or additive, which refers to 'the aggregated leadership behaviour of some, many or all of the members of an organization or an organizational sub-unit', leadership which is 'dispersed rather than concentrated' of leadership as concertive action, and secondly that distributed leadership is more than the sum of its parts. The other ideas he explores are:

'**Spontaneous collaboration**' concerning tasks. Leadership is evident in the interaction and relationships in which people with different skills, expertise and from different organizational levels come together to pool expertise and work together for the duration of the task. For example in the early years this may be projects in relation to language development of young children that would bring together the expertise of speech and language therapist, health visitor, teacher and outreach worker.

'**Shared role**' which emerges between two or more people, involving close joint working 'within an implicit framework of understanding' and emergent 'intuitive understandings'. For example when two people in a setting take on leading the delivery of a parenting programme for parents and carers and come from different professional backgrounds but share an understanding of the vision for the programme.

'**Institutionalization of structures**' of working together (concertive mechanisms), for example a committee. In children's centre terms this might be a steering group sharing the leadership of the centre across the partners involved in service delivery including users of the services.

Distributed leadership is not the same as delegation whether people are given specific jobs to complete. Distributed leadership allows people to take part in and ownership of the process of deciding the focus and then an active part in the leadership of organization.

Reflective task

Consider the organization in which you work. Are there examples of delegation of tasks? Is any of the leadership distributed allowing others to take a more active part in the leadership of the organization?

Summary of key ideas in this chapter

- Delegation is not the same as allowing others to develop their leadership skills, knowledge and experiences.
- Leaders need to consider ethical issues when working with other professionals and agree ground rules when working in groups.
- Distributed leadership offers opportunities to share and develop others' leadership skills in a variety of different ways.

Further reading

Clutterbuck, D. and Megginson, D., (1999). *Mentoring Executives and Directors*. Oxford: Butterworth-Heinemann

Parsloe, E. (1999). *The Manager as Coach and Mentor*. London: CIPD

Schön, D. (1983). The *Reflective Practitioner*. New York: Basic Books

Tuckman, B. (1965). Developmental sequence in small groups. *Psychological Bulletin*, 63, 384–399

Useful website

http://forms.ncsl.org.uk/mediastore/image2/distributedleadership_web/animation.htm (accessed 21.09.08)

9 Leadership and Careers

Chapter Outline

In this chapter we will look at the recruitment process and the ways in which others may perceive your actions in a current post and how this may affect your progression to a leadership role.

Standards that this chapter will help you explore are:

Early Years: S33, S34

Social Care: Functional area A, Functional area B, Functional area C, Functional area D, Functional area E and Functional area F

Children's centre leaders: 1. Leading learning and development, 2. Stronger families, stronger communities, 3. Being accountable and responsible, 4. Shaping the present and creating the future, 5. Managing the organization, 6. Building and strengthening teams

Teaching: Q5, Q6, Q32, Q33, C5, C6, C40, C41, P9, P10, E13, E14, E15, A2, A3, Shaping the future, Leading learning and teaching, Developing self and working with others, Managing the organization, Securing accountability, Strengthening community

By the end of this chapter you will:

- have explored different ways of thinking about opportunities to extend your career
- have explored the ideas behind career anchors
- have explored career patterns and paths including your own

Getting yourself noticed

If you have decided that you want a leadership role how do you go about getting yourself noticed in your organization? If you take on tasks over and above your current role are you seen by colleagues as trying to be different and risk alienating yourself from the rest of the staff group? If I am seen to be a good or excellent practitioner will leaders notice your skills and knowledge or will they want to keep you where you are as you are performing well and acting as a good role model for others? These are difficult questions to answer in some organizations as they are areas that are not discussed openly. If you are working in a learning and mentoring organization things are likely to be different. You may have supervision and/or appraisal sessions where you can raise your aspirations and talk about a plan for developing skills, knowledge and experiences that you will need to move you on to the next step towards a leader's role.

Other ways in which you might develop your leadership skills are to:

Work alongside others
Shadow leaders
Opportunities to share practice with others
Mentors within the organization
Mentors outside the organization

Impression management

In the past two decades or so we have finally laid to rest the notion of the linear career in all but the most bureaucratic of organizations. Today we are still concerned with progress through merit and ability, but some of our most talented people may not want to stretch themselves to the absolute limit and achieve the highest echelons of their employing organizations. Nevertheless as we have argued around the problematic issue of the impostor syndrome and how we can find many highly effective people whose self-image is one of being a less than peak performer we also have the other end of the scale. It is, we believe possible to find senior leaders who have no right to occupy the positions they do as they have completely overinflated personal perception of their own abilities. Somehow there are odd people who wreak havoc in organizations, clearly inappropriate for the position they hold yet are very skilled at presenting themselves in selection processes and interviews. It is argued that these people are experts in 'impression management'. They are Janis faced and can present one clearly defined set of behaviours to their bosses that makes them appear highly effective in their eyes. But to their staff they can be bullies and oppressive – the senior managers never ever seeing the product of their lack of leadership qualities and never being in a position to witness the negative behaviours they display to their staff.

This 'Impression Management' (Goffman 1959) is central to a crucial problem that we have when we think about a critical leadership issue – that how do we recruit and select leaders?

Reflective task

For a moment pause to think about who are truly the best (and perhaps only) predicators of a leaders performance?

Is it the staff?
The boss?
The peers?
Customers and service users?
Others, such as family friends or acquaintances?

A bit of a trick one this as we think you knew the answer all along. Peers are reasonable predictors of a leaders performance but the very best are staff. The poorest (apart from those such as family and friends that rarely see us in occupational settings) are bosses?

Can you think of why?

A fine balancing act?

Although it seems as though the times we thought of careers as a kind of stairway, moving from one level in the organizational hierarchy to the next as competence and experience was gained are now long past, we must remember that many of those in senior positions are there today because this was exactly what they experienced. We have gone some way to argue that tomorrow's leaders will have very different experiences on their journeys through working life.

Career anchors

One of the key aspects of thinking about our careers is work undertaken by Ed Schein (1996) *The Career Anchors.*

The original thinking behind this is that we as individuals choose a balance between particular organizational and personal issues when we are in the occupational world. It is best to think of this as a starting point as when we look at the total population of say doctors we do not find they are all there because they are driven by a need to do public good, nor is the total population of all who work as investment bankers driven by a need to make money. What we can postulate however is that there will be a significant percentage of people in these populations who are comfortable with these as their personal drivers.

Reflective task

Before looking at the nine career anchors think about the following questions:

What are the driving forces that took you into a career of working in the fields of education, child development and child support?

As a guess – think about what the driving forces might be for those who are your trusted work colleagues?

Think about the drivers of the people who are your senior leaders?

If you have trustees or elected members on your board think about what their personal career anchors and drivers are.

The nine career anchors

	Anchors	Primary drivers
1	Technical/functional competence	To be seen as being capable and competent at everything they do
2	Managerial competence	To be seen to thrive on responsibility
3	Security and stability	To avoid risk and be seen as reliable
4	Entrepreneurial creativity	To have control over the business and to invent new things
5	Autonomy and independence	To be seen as working to your own rules and prefer to work alone
6	Basic identity	To be seen to achieve an occupational identity – might like to wear a uniform
7	Service to others or a cause	To be seen as being driven to help and support other people
8	Power, influence and control	To be seen to have control over other people – different to managerial competence in that this anchor is about social and political control
9	Variety – or lifestyle	To be seen to have a wide range of talents – they may have portfolio careers

Source: Schein (1996)

For anyone in a leadership position it is vital to be fully aware of not just where you are personally 'anchored' in your career but to think through where others, especially your staff might be. Clearly the approach a leader has to have with a member of staff who is anchored in 'money' will have a different 'psychological contract' with their work as opposed to someone who is clearly anchored in doing social good.

What is important about Schein's (1996) work is that although there may be a debate over the content validity of the categories, many people report them as having very 'face validity'. In this we mean that when we think through the anchors we can see some of this in the people we know and work with and conversely we often see some of the people who we work with as being 'round pegs in square holes' – they do not appear to fit!

This is one of many explanations for the root causes of occupational stress; through peer, social or even family pressure many people make extreme compromises about their working lives and leaders have to deal with consequences of this. For many, the compromises are manageable but for others they can be the source of deep-rooted team and organizational problems. While we would never encourage the use of the career anchors as part of recruitment and selection exercises this work underscores the critical importance of recruiting the right people into occupational roles. To be competent is often not enough, we have to know how people fit into teams and work groups. Also, when we see opportunities to extend our careers we have to be aware of the compromises we may have to make if we were to get that attractive job!

What do we know about the careers of leaders?

The answer is surprisingly little – the biographies of many business leaders does however suggest that taking responsibility for people and projects, no matter how small early in your working life suggests that you are more likely to end your career in senior positions. But again as we have argued being in a senior position does not make you a leader. Often we see that people are promoted into senior leadership positions on the basis of their technical and functional abilities as opposed to their personal suitability to lead others. This is a topic that will not lie down for those involved in the industry of senior recruitment. Again we emphasize that the best determinant of any individual's leadership capacity and efficacy is not the boss but the staff, and until we can find a way of legitimately investigating how staff respond to the leadership approach of any individual there will remain a hole in the recruitment process that reliably informs recruiters' decisions.

Recruiting leaders – a recurring problem that will not go away

We set out the arguments in Chapter 3 about where we are in the debate about the differences and similarities of management and leadership. Clearly we feel that we can draw a very distinct line between the two, but when it comes to recruiting senior staff we expect both. In what appears to be a few short years we have come a long way in our thinking about the actual mechanisms and processes of recruitment – the days of the interview panel with a few, hopefully structured questions is mostly behind us, but if you are a candidate for a senior leadership role what can you do to present yourself as both a professional able to manage and a leader?

Reflective task

Think about your career to date. Have you planned for the progress that you have made or plan to make? What have been the deciding factors for you in applying for different posts? Have others

encouraged you to apply for posts? Jot down a few notes for yourself to consider how planned you career has been. Has family life had an impact on your career development? Have you stopped work to bring up children and perhaps therefore feel you have missed out on experiences and opportunities? How might you consider the skills developed in being at home could benefit an employer?

Job for life or changing career patterns

In nearly all post-World War II economies there was an expectation that employees would make few changes in their careers, the concept of 'job for life' was not an unrealizable prospect for many and progression was based upon a mixture of merit (irrespective of how poorly measured) and time served with the employer. Today this idea of 'careers' may not be totally obsolete, but it is certainly less common than it was a working generation ago.

For many the idea of a career is more akin to a game of snakes and ladders, there is 360 degree movement and a casual conversation with colleagues for most illustrates this, we find that leaders often make very reasoned decisions to move sideways and even backwards to accumulate experience or to place themselves in positions where the careers can be advantaged. It may be that we need robust economic conditions to do this where risk taking in careers is low, periods with lower levels of rewards and benefits can be sustained in the belief that placing yourself in different contexts with lower rewards will have a pay-off at a later date. In many ways fixed-term contract work has made this more of a reality for many, where a choice is made to undertake a role for a fixed period to position oneself for a move to a more advanced and rewarding position at a later date.

Careers therefore may fall into the following categorization, and it would be significant to look at early years settings as an emergent occupational category to establish if there is a predominant pattern to careers.

Linear – progressive steps in an established hierarchy

Key questions

What factors are determining hierarchical structures in early years settings?

To what extent is size of setting, location and governance factors impacting upon organizational designs that create career opportunities for leaders in the early years?

Spiral careers

Patterns become established where related occupational areas have an element of transferability of perceived skills, attributes and competence. Moving through social care to primary education to early years leadership for example.

Key questions

Are there recognized, related occupational groupings that are valued and complementary becoming established for those employed in early years settings?

Are there contrary indicators where experience in other settings is becoming established as dead ends or career limiting factors?

Transitory careers

Where individuals seek out a career composed of varied experiences in a seemingly patternless and opportunistic timeline.

Key questions

Are there any inbuilt prejudices building up that prevent talented people from gaining access into the early years as a profession?

What are the implications for equalities issues where sections of the community may be disadvantaged as they have by necessity taken employment in a variety of settings or have taken work opportunities in economically challenged locations on an ad hoc basis?

Expert careers

Accumulation and refinement of experiences, skills and capabilities in a planned and logical sequence.

Reflective task

Are there mechanisms developing that standardize and define what particular skills, capabilities and work experiences are seen as valuable or even essential to be an effective senior leader in the early years?

Again, are there any structurally discriminatory elements to the way that emergent leaders can gain experience and develop expertise?

Richardson (1996) looked at women in accountancy careers and highlighted the structural and perceptual challenges that women are exposed to and highlighted the gender differences in the perception of what a career actually is. For men careers were about logical and structured progression and accruing power and responsibility, but for women careers were more about self-fulfilment and building competence and capability. This suggests that in peer groups the needs for recognition could be very different, and as we can see that early years workers are dominated by one gender this may have an important influence on how leadership potential is seen. An issue made doubly problematic if there are severe gender imbalances in recruitment processes.

At this stage it is worth looking again at the actual mechanisms that are used in the recruitment process for leaders in early years settings. There is a breadth of literature on multi-inequalities in the workplace but a report by the Women's Leadership Network (WLN 2007) highlighted that depth of imbalance in the workplace.

Women were over-represented in certain sectors in first line supervisory roles, but –
Women were severely under-represented in senior leadership roles, and –
Black and minority ethnic (BME) groups were under represented at all levels outside positions of responsibility.

While we have a sound basis for legislation that is anti-discriminatory there are seemingly structural issues deeply embedded that consistently produce highly skewed results in the data around gender, disability, age and ethnicity in employment.

Reflective task

Draw a career timeline for yourself – start with your last years at school and list the career aspirations you had then, move onto your first jobs and how, if all your career aspirations changed? Keep the timeline going up to your current position and review your present career aspirations. To what extent have they changed, if at all?

Go back to the above career typology and explore to what extent your personal career either conforms or challenges the typology?

Drawing this together we can see that there are many leaders in early years who have arrived here through many and varied paths. In looking at careers we need to go back to the starting point and ask does leadership become a product of what has gone before or is it a way of determining what is to come. We are struck that with so many leaders with various backgrounds there is a critical need to network this experience for the population of professionals in the field before that experience is dissipated.

Summary of key ideas in this chapter

- Decisions are often made through 'impression management'
- Career anchors can be a useful way of exploring your own career
- The traditional patterns of a single career for life are changing and people often have varied career patterns and paths to leadership positions

Further reading

Goffman, E. (1959). *The Presentation of Self in Everyday Life*. Doubleday: Garden City, New York

Rosener, J. B. (1995). *American's Competitive Secret: Utilizing Women as a Management Strategy.* New York: Oxford University Press

Schein, E. (1996). *Career Anchors – Discovering your Real Values*. Oxford: Pfeiffer

So What Now?

Post-industrial society has a long-standing concern for the care, development and education of its younger members. Children's policy from successive UK governments has at least recognized that the provision of rich, sustaining environments from post-natal stages onwards have an impact upon social measures at later stages. The argument has centred more upon the resource and positioning of these services and not on the important place they have in wider educational, care and social settings. Most politicians and policy makers from across the piste agree that early years provision is a staple and fewer see it as optional or discretionary. This explosion on the focus and attention on early years provision has coincided with a crescendo of debate on leadership. Therefore early years leaders have found themselves at an interesting confluence. Reviewing the approach to leadership development in other sectors of the UK public economy such as the NHS, Local Government, Police and Fire and Rescue leads us to voice our concern that leaders do need to be supported, but we must be very careful not to fall into the traps that others have. The days of the large-scale leadership development interventions into parts of the public sector appear to have now gone. Government have put large amounts of pump priming resource into leadership development and then looked for immediate impact. In one case we can point to the policy stakeholders at a national level actually expecting participants on a yearlong leadership development programme to be in a position to immediately apply for the most senior jobs on completion of the programme. What we know as both developers and at times being participants ourselves is that it is a 'slow burn'. This is not say those large-scale leadership development initiatives were of no use, clearly they were; it is just that the intentions the stakeholders had for them might have been a little misplaced.

Leaders need to learn, reflect, couple that reflection to experience and it may be years before the real impact of a development programme can take effect. 'Feeling ready' to take on senior leadership positions sounds very imprecise, but it is possibly the most realistic starting point for the best leaders.

Another concern that has been highlighted in looking at the leadership issues for the early years is the persistent trend for the universal set of transferable leadership competencies. We have seen this trend begin to impact upon early years settings. Where early years settings are closely tied into a corporate sense of a local authority there has been a wish to envelope the setting in the corporate blanket of the organization. Leaders and those in governance have been encouraged to participate in development around the corporate leadership competencies. This may be okay at one level, but it does have the tendency to reduce leadership to the lowest common denominator and as we have seen brings an element of compliance that does not always sit easily with the dynamic nature of leadership.

In your journey of exploration as a leader it is perhaps the journey that is important and not the destination. You will come across people who will offer you a false destination. 'We have the research to show that our model of leadership is more reliable than others.' The market for leadership development is not quite a bandwagon but care needs to be exercised when purchasing from the marketplace. Remember, the market for leadership development has no regulation to it.

Another stand out feature of our tour of leadership in the early years explodes more myths. Leadership development does not always require a large cheque to be signed. So many stories of highly motivated and clearly able leaders who invest in their (and others') leadership development through simple yet massively engaging and inexpensive processes illustrate the possibilities. The way they have chosen to run their meetings, the discussions they found time to have with others or simply just going to see other settings and conducting basic contextual research and a surprising number who are in carefully chosen mentoring relationship point to leadership development activity that is healthy and very outcome focused. They have engaged in seeking feedback on their performance from a wide range of people who experience their leadership in different ways which has given them insights into the ways in which they operate in their settings.

One conclusion is that we can see some fit for many of the paradigms from other professional starting points for the leadership in early years settings. However with so many variable settings a key issue is that leadership flourishes where there is a strong recognition that these are the organizations that reflect the uniqueness of localized need and character. Exceptional leaders place their services to early years users in a localized context. They create a setting with a unique reflection of not what the users require but what the communities they serve require. We feel that where those external to the setting place early years somewhere between social care and education with a little bit of a health theme thrown in are missing the point in relation to developing truly multi-agency partnership working. Leaders are drawn from many backgrounds and careers, but they are setting the agenda for the continuing development of early years in a changing context, which makes this role a challenging and complex one. Existing leaders and aspiring ones require support to develop their skills, knowledge and effectiveness in appropriate ways for the services to children and their families. It has not been possible in one publication to cover all the potential aspects of early years leadership development but we hope this book will add to the potential starting points for leaders in the early years. We recognize that this area is an emergent and dynamic environment that does not benefit from the traditions that other related professional groups do. In exploring this topic we have drawn renewed enthusiasm from many examples of good practice.

Appendix of Professional Standards

Professional standards

Day care	Early Years Practitioner Status (EYPS) CWDC (2007)
The National Standards for day care include the following about the leader of the setting. The manager has at least a level 3 qualification appropriate to the post. In addition: the manager has at least 2 years experience of working in a day care setting; all managers, staff and volunteers are suitable, both mentally and physically, to care for children; all managers, staff and volunteers have the appropriate experience, skills and ability to do their jobs.	Knowledge and understanding Effective practice Relationships with children Communicating and working in partnership with families and carers Teamwork and collaboration Professional development. Candidates for EYPS must demonstrate through their practice that a secure knowledge and understanding of the above areas underpins their own practice and informs their leadership of others. The full standards can be found on the following web reference http://www.cwdcouncil.org.uk/assets/0000/0612/EYPS_Guidance_to_Standards_Jan07.pdf. In relation to leadership the following standards are the most pertinent for this book. Teamwork and collaboration Candidates for EYPS must demonstrate that they: **S33** Establish and sustain a culture of collaborative and cooperative working between colleagues **S34** Ensure that colleagues working with them understand their role and are involved appropriately in helping children to meet planned objectives **S35** Influence and shape the policies and practices of the setting and share in collective responsibility for their implementation **S36** Contribute to the work of a multi-professional team and, where appropriate, coordinate and implement agreed programmes and interventions on a day-to-day basis

Social care

McDonnell and Zutshi (2006) have mapped leadership and management standards for social care. http://www.topssengland.net/files/prod3%202edn%2006webedn(1)(1).pdf (accessed 21.09.08)

The key areas are as follows:

A	Managing self and personal skills
B	Providing direction
C	Facilitating change
D	Working with people
E	Using resources
F	Achieving results

They subdivide these areas from the National Health Service (NHS) standards into generic, specialist and partnership skills.

A key to the specialist standards mentioned in the table is as follows:

AGA: = Advice Guidance and Advocacy

CJ: = Community Justice

DANOS: = Drugs and Alcohol (Skills for Health, incorporated into HSC units)

H: = Housing

H+S: = Health and Safety

HSC: = Health and Social Care

L+D: = Learning and Development

NU: = New Unit

REC: = Recruitment and Employment

SW: = Social Work

YJ: = Youth Justice

YW: = Youth Work

SA = Skills Active MH = Mental health (Skills for Health)

Also the following categories have been used:

NHSKSF = NHS Knowledge and Skills Framework Dimensions, e.g. G1:1 = General number: level C1:1 = Core number: level

RMA = Registered Manager Adults

RMRCC = Registered Manager Residential Child Care

PQ CC = Post Qualifying Child Care

VSNTO = Voluntary Sector National Training Organisation Functional Map of Managing Volunteers

CBLD = Community Based Learning and Development (PAULO) NSH = National Standards for Headteachers, DfES (2004b)

[NB: distinction betwenn NSH and NHS]

Functional Area A: Managing self and personal skills

NSH Developing self and working with others

Generic standards	Specialist standards	Partnership standards
A1 Manage your own resources – to make sure you have the personal resources (knowledge, understanding, skills and time) to undertake your work role and review your performance against agreed objectives. It also covers identifying and undertaking activities to develop your knowledge, skills and understanding where gaps have been identified	**AGA20** Evaluate and develop own contribution to the service **SA:A310** Develop your own resources **SW:14** Manage and be accountable for your own work **HSC:E1.1** Reflect upon and develop own practice using supervision and support systems **NHSKSF C2.1 Personal and people development** – contribute to own personal development	
A2 Manage your own resources and professional development to achieve your work objectives and career and personal goals. You need to understand your work role and how it fits into the overall vision and objectives of the organisation, whilst also understanding what is driving you in terms of your values, career and wider personal aspirations. Identifying and addressing gaps in your skills, knowledge and understanding is an essential part of this unit.	**RMA:RG6** Take responsibility for your business performance and the continuing development of self and others **SW:14** Manage and be accountable for your own work **HSC:E1.1** Reflect upon and develop own practice using supervision and support systems **DANOS:AC2** Make use of supervision **RMRCC:12** Take responsibility for the continuing professional development of self and others **NHSKSF C2:4** Develop oneself and others in areas of practice	
A3 Develop your personal networks – based on principles of reciprocity and confidentiality to support both your current and future work	**NHSKSF C1:2 Communication** – communicate with a range of people on a range of matters **NHSKSF C 1.4 Communication** – develop and maintain communication with people on complex matters, issues and ideas and/or in complex situations	

NHS LQF Personal qualities: Self awareness – knows own strengths and limitations and understands own emotions and the impact of behaviour on others in diverse situations **Self management** – able to manage own emotions and be resilient in a range of complex and demanding situations **Personal integrity** – a strongly held sense of commitment to openness, honesty, inclusiveness and high standards in undertaking the leadership role **Self belief** – has inner confidence to succeed and can overcome obstacles to achieve the best outcomes for service improvement **Drive for improvement** – a deep motivation to improve the performance in the health service

Functional Area B: Providing Direction

NSH Leading Learning and Teaching
NSH Shaping the future
NSH Securing accountability

Generic standards	Specialist standards	Partnership standards
B1 Develop and implement operational plans for your area of responsibility – which will contribute to achieving the objectives set out in the strategic business plan **Also see B3**	**RMRCC:19 RMA:BDA2** Develop your plans for the business **SA:A11** Assist the organisation to develop and implement policies **SNTO:A4** Develop plans to meet your organisation's goals **DANOS:BC1** Develop, negotiate and agree proposals to offer services and products **DANOS:BA3 HSC439** Contribute to the development of organisational policy and practice **MH:K2** Develop and agree priorities and objectives for meeting the mental health needs of the population	**SW:6** Prepare, produce, implement and evaluate plans with individuals, families, carers, groups and communities **H57** Consult on an agree objectives for the service
B2 Map the environment in which your business operates – have a clear and up-to-date picture of the environment and produce information, which could be used for planning and operational purposes. The 'environment' includes the 'external' operating environment – for example, customers and their needs, market trends, new technologies and methods, legislation, and the activities of competitors and partners. It also includes the 'internal' operating environment – for example resources available to, and the culture of, the organisation	**MH:K1** Identify trends and changes in the mental health needs of a population and the effectiveness of meeting those needs **SA:A42** Provide information to inform decision making **HSC:48** Use information to take critical decisions **RMA:D4** Provide information to support decision making **MH:M5** Monitor and review changes in the environments and practices to promote mental health	**MH:L1** Determine the concerns and priorities of communities about mental health needs **MH:M1** Assess how environments and practices can be maintained and improved to promote mental health **MH:M2** Facilitate collaborative action by stakeholders to improve environments and practice to promote mental health

B3 Develop a strategic business plan for your organisation – develop and reach agreement with colleagues and other stakeholders on a plan, which provides a clear sense of direction, and long-term plans that will help them move in that direction. Strategy is all about developing that vision and producing flexible plans to make the vision a reality. **Also see B1**	**DANOS BA1** Review and enhance your organisation's strategic position **DANOS:BA2** Establish strategies to guide the work of your organisation **HSC440 VSNTO:A1 SA:B218** Contribute to the development of your organisation's strategy **MH:K3** Develop, implement and improve strategies to meet the mental health needs of a population **MH:K4** Develop, monitor, evaluate and review services for addressing mental health needs	**NHSKSF C1. 4 Communication** – develop and maintain communication with people on complex matters, issues and ideas and/or in complex situations (level 4) **NHSKSF C4:4 Service Improvement** – work in partnership with others to develop, take forward and evaluate direction, policies and strategies **VSNTO:B3** Develop relationships with individuals and organisations that can support your volunteering strategy **NHSKSF G7:4 Capacity and capability** – work in partnership with others to develop and sustain capacity and capability **MH:L2** Work with groups and communities to develop policies, strategies and services to improve mental health and address mental health needs
B4 Put the strategic plan into action- – transforming plans into action, 'selling' the strategy to others involved in putting it into practice, having agreed standards for measuring success, carefully monitoring the implementation and making adjustments along the way.	**SA:A11** Assist the organisation to develop and implement policies **VSNTO:A3** Develop organisational structures and systems to support volunteering **DANOS:BA6** Manage the development and direction of the provision	**AGA:37** Negotiate and maintain service agreements **DANOS:BB1** Promote your organisation and its services to stakeholders
B5 Provide leadership for your team – to provide direction, motivate and support them to achieve both team and personal work objectives. **See B6 and B7**	**DANOS:BF5 HSC:451** Lead teams to support a quality provision **DANOS:BF12 HSC:451** Lead and motivate volunteers **HSC:C1.1** Contribute to the effectiveness of teams **RMA:D2 DANOS:BI3** Facilitate meetings	
B6 Provide leadership in your area of responsibility – to provide direction, motivate and support people to achieve the vision and objectives for the area of your responsibility. **See B5 and B7**	**RMRCC: 2 HSC:D1.4 DANOS:BA6** Manage the development and direction of the provision **RMRCC: 9 PQCC:D** Contribute to the development of services, policies and practice which optimise life chances for all children and young people	
B7 Provide leadership for your organisation – to provide direction to people to enable, inspire, motivate and support them to achieve what the organisation has set out to do and apply different styles of leadership appropriate to different people and situations. **See B5 and B6**		

(Continued)

Functional Area B: Providing Direction (Cont'd)

Generic standards	Specialist standards	Partnership standards
B8 Ensure compliance with legal, regulatory, ethical and social requirements – obeying the law in key areas such as health and safety, employment, finance and corporate law, as well as professional and ethical frameworks	**RMA:F6 SA:A58** Monitor compliance with quality systems **RMA:A2 DANOS:BC2** Manage activities to meet requirements **DANOS:BA5** Support effective governance **SW:20** Manage complex ethical issues, dilemmas and conflicts **HSC:E2.2** Support and challenge workers on specific aspects of their practice **VSNTO: F11** Report to external agencies	**MH:N1** Enable workers and agencies to work collaboratively
B9 Developing the culture of your organisation – 'the way we do things around here' – which fits with the overall mission and strategy. The culture of an organisation is based on assumptions and values which influence the way people behave towards each other and customers, and how they relate to their work	**RMRCC: 1 HSC:48** Demonstrate a style of leadership that ensures an organisational culture of open and participatory management practice **HSC:E2.1** Promote the values and principles underpinning best practice **YW: F4** Promote a culture to safeguard the welfare of young people **NHSKSF C5.4 Quality** – develop a culture that improves quality	**YJ:B102** Contribute to developing and maintaining cultures and strategies in which children and young people are respected and valued as individuals **MH:M3** Contribute to developing and maintaining cultures and strategies in which people are respected and valued as individuals
B10 Manage risk – taking the lead in establishing and operating an effective risk management process across your organisation. This involves systematically identifying, evaluating and prioritising potential risks and communicating information to enable appropriate actions to be taken. It also involves developing an organisational culture in which individuals are risk aware but are not afraid of taking decisions and undertaking activities which involve acceptable levels of risk. **Also see E6**	**H&S: E** Promote a health and safety culture **SW:12** Assess and manage risks to individuals, families, carers, groups and communities **YJ:B103** Evaluate risk of abuse, failure to protect and harm to self and others **HSC:B1.2** Assess and act upon risk of danger to individuals and others **CBLD: 12** Challenge policies, practice and failures in the system **NHSKSF C3.4 Health, safety and security** – maintain and develop an environment and culture that improves health, safety and security	

B11 Promote equality of opportunity and diversity in your area of responsibility – this is intended to go beyond compliance with equality legislation towards a situation where there is awareness and active commitment to the need to ensure equality of opportunity and the benefits of diversity. **Also see B12**	**RMA:O3 MH:M4** Develop, maintain and evaluate systems and structures to promote the rights, responsibilities and diversity of people **YW:D2** Work in ways that promote equality of opportunity, participation and responsibility **NHSKSF C6.3 Dimension Core 6: Equality, diversity** Promote equality and diversity **HSC:452** Contribute to the development, maintenance and evaluation of systems to promote the rights, responsibilities, equality and diversity of individuals **MH:O9** Promote people's equality and respect for diversity
B12 Promote equality of opportunity and diversity in your organisation – taking a lead in actively promoting quality of opportunity and diversity by ensuring policies and action plans exist and are communicated and implemented across the organisation. It also involves monitoring and reviewing progress to identify further actions and changes to practice. **Also see B11**	**RMA:O3 MH:M4** Develop, maintain and evaluate systems and structures to promote the rights, responsibilities and diversity of people **NHSKSF C6.4 Equality and diversity** – develop a culture that promotes equality and values diversity

NHS LQF Setting direction: Broad scanning – taking the time to gather information from a wide range of sources **Intellectual flexibility** – the facility to embrace and cut through ambiguity and complexity and to be open to creativity in leading and developing services **Seizing the future** – being prepared to take action now to shape and implement a vision for the future development of the service **Drive for results** – a strong commitment to making service performance improvements and a determination to achieve positive service outcomes for users **Political astuteness** – showing commitment and ability to understand diverse interest groups and power bases within organisations and the wider community, and the dynamic between them, so as to lead health services more effectively **Personal qualities: Drive for improvement** – a deep motivation to improve the performance in the health service **Delivering the service: Leading change through people** – communicating the vision and rationale for change and modernization, and engaging and facilitating others to work collaboratively to achieve real change

Functional area C: Facilitating change

NHS shaping the future

Generic standards	Specialist standards	Partnership standards
C1 Encourage innovation in your team – encouraging people to improve current services and ways of doing things by developing a climate where people feel able to think creatively about practice, systems and processes. Also see **C2** and **C3**	**RMA:A4** Contribute to improvements at work **L+D:9** Create a climate that promotes learning **NHSKSF G2:1** Development and innovation. Appraise concepts, models, methods, practices, products and equipment developed by others	
C2 Encourage innovation in your area of responsibility to support the identification and practical implementation of ideas, primarily from people in your area of responsibility, for improving existing services and developing new services. Also see **C1** and **C3**	**NHSKSF G2:2** Development and innovation – contribute to developing, testing and reviewing new concepts, models, methods, practices, products and equipment **NHSKSF G2:3** Development and innovation – test and review new concepts, models, methods, practices, products and equipment	
C3 Encourage innovation in your organisation – provide encouragement and support to identify and implement ideas from people within but also to look outside the organisation to develop new services and improve existing services. Also see **C2** and **C3**	**NHSKSF G2.4** Development and innovation – develop new and innovative concepts, models, methods, practices, products and equipment	**NHSKSF C4.4** Service improvement – work in partnership with others to develop, take forward and evaluate direction, policies and strategies **HSC: C2.1** Develop joint working agreements and practices
C4 Lead change – providing a lead within the overall organisation or part of an organisation for a specific change or a wider programme of change. Involves selling the vision in terms of what the change is intended to achieve and supporting those involved in the practicalities of making the vision a reality. See **C5** and **C6**	**NHSKSF C1.4** Communication – develop and maintain communication with people on complex matters, issues and ideas and/or in complex situations **DANOS:BF5** Lead teams to provide a quality service	**MH:N7** Lead the development, implementation and improvement of interagency services for addressing mental health needs

C5 Plan change – developing a strategy to achieve the required change, taking note of barriers, risks and the need to put appropriate monitoring and communication systems in place. See **C4** and **C6**		
C6 Implement change – implementing the strategy and associated plans for a specific change or programme of change; putting in place the necessary resources and supporting mechanisms, including monitoring and communications, to turn the 'vision' into a practical reality. See **C4** and **C5**	**DANOS:BC3** Manage change in organisational activities	**SW:5** Interact with individuals, families, carers, groups and communities to achieve change and development and to improve life opportunities

NHA LQF Setting direction: **Drive for results** – a strong commitment to making service performance improvements and a determination to achieve positive service outcomes for users **Intellectual flexibility** – the facility to embrace and cut through ambiguity and complexity and to be open to creativity in leading and developing services **Delivering the service: Leading change through people –** communicating the vision and rationale for change and modernisation, and engaging and facilitating others to work collaboratively to achieve real change **Personal qualities: Drive for improvement** – a deep motivation to improve performance in the health service

Functional area D: Working with people

NSH Developing self and working with others

NSH Securing accountability

Generic standards	Specialist standards	Partnership standards
D1 Develop productive working relationships with colleagues in your own and other organisations that are effective in delivering the work of the organization. **Also see D2**	**RMA:HSCL 4U9** Develop productive working relationships **SA:A314** Create, maintain and develop an effective environment **YW:D2** Manage your work and create effective work relationships	**SW:17** Work with multidisciplinary and multi-organisational teams, networks and systems **DANOS:BI6 MH:N3** Develop and sustain effective working relationships with staff in other agencies
D2 Developing productive working relationships with colleagues and stakeholders in order to ensure that both the interests of the organisation and the interests of stakeholders are addressed. Requires awareness of who the relevant stakeholders are and what influence they have in the organisation. **Also see D1**	**NHSKSF C1:4 Communication** – establish and maintain effective communication with various individuals	**RMA:SC15** Develop and sustain arrangements for joint working between workers and agencies **YJ:D301** Enable workers and agencies to work collaboratively **YJ:D302** Develop, sustain and evaluate collaborative approaches with others **YW:E3** Build and maintain partnership working **DANOS:B12** Develop joint working arrangements and practices and review their effectiveness
D3 Recruit, select and keep colleagues to ensure the most suitable people are employed (directly or indirectly) by the organisation.	**RMA:C8 SA:A311 DANOS:BF3** Select personnel for activities **DANOS:BF2** Develop, implement and evaluate strategies and policies for recruiting and managing volunteers **RMRCC:10 SA:A312** Contribute to the selection, recruitment and retention of staff to develop a quality service **DANOS:BF10** Contribute to the recruitment and placement of volunteers **NHSKSF G6:4** People management – Plan, develop, monitor and review the recruitment, deployment and management of people	

D4 Plan the workforce – taking a lead in identifying the workforce requirements of your organisation and how these will be satisfied. Planning the number and type of people who work for the organisation; considering strategic plans to determine whether the workforce should be expanded, maintained or contracted, ensuring the appropriate mix of people to deliver organisational objectives.	**DANOS:BF1** Develop a strategy and plan to provide all people resources for the organisation **DANOS:BF9** Redeploys personnel and make redundancies **NHSKSF G6:4** Plan, develop, monitor and review the recruitment, deployment and management of people
D5 Allocate and check work in your team – allocate work effectively and fairly among team members, check progress and quality to ensure level or standards or performance are being met. **Also see D6**	**RMA:C13 HSC:444** Manage the performance of teams and individuals **VSNTO:D1 DANOS:BF11** Plan, organise and manage the work of volunteers **HSC (draft unit – product 6)** Manage effective supervision **RMCC:13** Assess candidates' performance through observation **RMRCC:14** Assess candidates using a range of methods **DANOS:BF7** Respond to poor performance in your team **DANOS:BF8 SA:A315** Deal with poor performance in your team **NHSKSF G6:1** People management – supervise people's work **NHSKSF G6:2** People management – plan, allocate and supervise the work of a team

(*Continued*)

Functional area D: Working with people (Cont'd)

Generic standards	Specialist standards	Partnership standards
D6 Allocate and monitor the progress and quality of work in your area of responsibility – plan and allocate work to individuals or teams; monitor progress and quality to ensure standards of performance are being met; and review and update plans in the light of developments. Also see **D5**	**HSC446** Manage a dispersed workforce to meet the needs and preferences of individuals at home **HSC** (draft unit – product 6) Manage effective supervision **RMRCC:15** Conduct internal quality assurance of the assessment process **SA:A39** Internally verify the assessment process **NHSKSF C5:4 Quality** – develop a culture that improves quality **NHSKSF G6:3 People management** – coordinate and delegate work and review people's performance **MH:O8** Support and challenge workers on specific aspects of their practice	**HSC:C2.5** Support inter-disciplinary teams to develop and implement individual programmes of care **MH:O7** Support and challenge teams and agencies on specific areas of their practice

D7 Provide learning opportunities for colleagues to improve performance with emphasis on developing a learning culture within the organisation so that colleagues take responsibility for their own learning and are supported in this by the organisation.	**RMA:C10 DANOS:BF4 RMRCC:11** Develop teams and individuals to enhance performance **MH:O4** Contribute to the development of the knowledge and practice of others **RMRCC:16** Support competence achieved in the workplace **CBLD:9** Developing and supporting learning mentor networks **L+D:17** Evaluate and improve learning and development programmes **L+D:16** Monitor and review progress with learners **DANOS:AC3** Contribute to the development of the knowledge and practice of others **NHSKSF G1:2** Learning and development – enable people to learn and develop **NHSKSF C2:2** Personal and people development – develop own skills and knowledge and provide information to others to help their development **NHSKSF G1:3** Plan, deliver and review interventions to enable people to learn and develop

NHS LQF Delivering the service: Collaborative working – being committed to working and engaging constructively with internal and external stakeholders **Effective and strategic influencing** – being able and prepared to adopt a number of ways to gain support and influence diverse parties, with the aim of securing health improvements **Empowering others** – striving to facilitate others' contributions and to share leadership, nurturing capability and long-term development of others **Holding to account** – the strength of resolve to hold others to account for agreed targets and to be held accountable for delivering a high level of service

Functional Area E: Using resources

NSH Managing the organisation

Generic standards	Specialist standards	Partnership standards
E1 Manage a budget for a defined area of responsibility, which includes preparing, agreeing and monitoring a budget and taking action when there are unforeseen developments.	**SW:16** Manage, present and share records and reports	
E2 Manage finance in your area of responsibility managing money to achieve goals and aims, drawing on internal or external financial expertise if necessary.	**NHSKSF G4:3** Financial management – coordinate, monitor and review the use of financial resources **NHSKSF G4:4** Financial management – plan, implement, monitor and review the acquisition, allocation and management of financial resources **NHSKSF G3:3** Procurement and commissioning – commission and procure products, equipment, services, systems and facilities **NHSKSF G7:3** Capacity and capability – contribute to developing and sustaining capacity and capability **RMA:B3 SA:A23 DANOS:BG4** Manage the use of financial resources **H:49** Contribute to the financial management of your organisation	**NHSKSF G7:4** Capacity and capability – work in partnership with others to develop and sustain capacity and capability
E3 Obtain additional finance for the organisation – identifying and obtaining the finance needed to achieve strategic goals and objectives, drawing on the expertise of financial specialists as appropriate.	**DANOS:BG1** Secure financial resources for your organisation's plans **DANOS:BG2** Plan and coordinate fund raising for the organisation **H:53** Identify and access funding **VSNTO:F3** Obtain funds to realise your organisation's volunteering policies and plans	

E4 Promote the use of technology within your organisation – make sure the organisation assesses the use of technology, gets the technology it needs, uses it in the best way possible and improving it as necessary. Technology might mean information or communications technology, equipment, machinery and so on. You are not expected to be a technology specialist but you would be expected to be able to need to work effectively with specialists.	**VSNTO:F10** Manage information and knowledge **N1** Manage systems for information, knowledge and communications **NHSKSF G3:2** Procurement and commissioning – assist in commissioning, procuring and monitoring goods and/or services **DANOS:BE1** Establish information management and communication systems
E5 Ensure your own actions reduce risks to health and safety by identifying hazards and evaluating risks in the workplace and taking action to put things right.	**HSC:B3.1** Contribute to the prevention and management of abusive and aggressive behaviour **SW:9** Address behaviour which represents a risk to individuals, families, carers, groups and individuals
E6 Ensure health and safety requirements are met in your area of responsibility by developing a culture that ensures safety considerations are firmly embedded in the planning and decision making processes within your remit. **Also see B10 and E7**	**SA:C216** Plan for safety of people attending an event **SA:C217** Ensure the safety of people attending an event **RMRCC:6 HSC:49** Develop and maintain an environment which safeguards and protects children and young people **H&S:E** Promote a health and safety culture **NHSKSF C3.4** Health, safety and security – maintain and develop an environment and culture that improves health, safety and security
E7 Ensure an effective organisational approach to health and safety by leading the overall approach to contribute to the well being and productivity of staff; decrease risks; improve the organisation's reputation and ensure legislative requirements are met. **Also see B10 and E6**	**NHSKSF C3:4** Health, safety and security – develop a working environment and culture that improves health, safety and security **(level 4)** **H&S:E** Promote a health and safety culture **RMRCC:18** Develop and maintain healthy and safe working practices and environment **DANOS:BD4** Promote, monitor and maintain health, safety and security in the working environment

NHS LQF Delivering the service: Holding to account – the strength of resolve to hold others to account for agreed targets and to be held accountable for delivering a high level of service **Setting direction: Intellectual flexibility** – the facility to embrace and cut through ambiguity and complexity and to be open to creativity in leading and developing services

Functional Area F: Achieving Results

NSH Managing the organization
NSH Securing accountability
NSH Strengthening the community

Generic standards	Specialist standards	Partnership standards
F1 Manage a project – taking responsibility for leading, planning, monitoring and controlling implementation of a project to ensure it meets its objectives and is completed to the satisfaction of the key stakeholders.	**RMA:SNH4U1** Develop programmes, projects and plans **SA:B219** Contribute to project planning and preparation **VSNTO:F2** Manage projects involving volunteers **MH:O3** Project manage action targeted at addressing mental health issues **H:54** Identify and select contractors to deliver projects **SA:B220** Contribute to project closure	
F2 Manage a programme of complementary projects leading and managing a specific programme of dissimilar projects, which are independent but interdependent upon each other. Taken together these projects will contribute to the achievement of a bigger strategic aim	**SA:B219** Coordinate the running of projects **NHSKSF G5:3** Services and project management – prioritise and manage the ongoing work of services and/or projects **NHSKSF G5:4** Services and project management – plan, coordinate and monitor the delivery of services and/or projects	
F3 Manage business processes to ensure the organisation delivers outputs that meet customer and/or stakeholder, organisational and legal requirements	**RMRCC:20 DANOS:BG3** Determine the effective use of resources **RMA:1 DANOS:BC5** Manage service, which meets the best possible outcomes for the individual **RMRCC:4** Manage and contribute to child care practice in group living **DANOS:BE2** Receive, analyse, process and store information	

F4 Develop and review a framework for marketing – taking informed, basic business decisions to develop a framework which describes the organisation's customers and how it will market and promote its services.	**DANOS:BB1 HSC:437 CSNTO:F1** Promote your organisation and its services to stakeholders **NHSKSF G8:2** Public relations and marketing – undertake public relations and marketing activities **NHSKSF G8:4** Public relations and marketing – plan, develop, monitor and review public relations and marketing for a service/organisation
F5 Resolve customer service problems by looking at options and resolving both reported and potential problems.	**H&S:F** Investigate and evaluate incidents and complaints in the workplace
F6 Monitor and solve customer service problems by sorting them out efficiently and effectively and changing systems to avoid repeated problems.	
F7 Support customer service improvements – support the organisation in making changes and present them positively to customers. Also present your own ideas for improvement based on listening to customers.	**PQCC:C1** Work with children and young people's networks to achieve optimal outcomes

(*Continued*)

Functional Area F Achieving Results (Cont'd)

Generic standards	Specialist standards	Partnership standards
F8 Work with others to improve customer services – communicate and agree how to positively work together to provide an effective service and monitor how joint performance has changed and improved services	**DANOS:AG1** Plan and agree service responses which meet individual's identified needs and circumstances **RMA:SC20** Contribute to the provision of effective physical, social and emotional environments for group care	**NHSKSF C1:4** Communication – develop and maintain communication with people on complex matters, issues and ideas and/or in complex situations **NHSKSF C4:4** Service improvement – work in partnership with others to develop, take forward and evaluate direction, policies and strategies **NHSKSF G7:4** Capacity and capability – work in partnership with others to develop and sustain capacity and capability **H32** Develop and maintain joint working to meet individual customer needs **YW:E3** Build and maintain partnership work **MH:N2** Develop, sustain and evaluate collaborative work with others **MH:O6** Work with teams and agencies to review progress and performance and identify next steps **PQCC:C2** Liase and work with other professionals and agencies to achieve optimal outcomes **RMRCC:7** Work with parents, families, carers and significant others to achieve optimal outcomes for children and young people **RMRCC:8** Undertake and /or co-ordinate work with networks, communities and agencies to achieve optimal outcomes for children and young people **MH:L5** Work with individuals and families to develop services to improve their mental health and address their mental health needs

F9 Build your organisation's understanding of its market and customers, ensuring relevant and reliable information is constantly available and shared to aid decision-making.	**RMA:D4** Provide information to support decision making **SA:A57** Provide advice and support for the development and implementation of quality policies **NHSKSF G2:1** Development and innovation – appraise concepts, models, methods, practices, products and equipment developed by others	**RMA:SNH4U4** Promote the interests of client groups in the community
F10 Develop a customer-focused organisation, providing the lead and support for the creation and maintenance of a customer-focused organisational culture.	**H:48** Develop and maintain procedures for customer participation **YW:C3** Review progress and evaluate opportunities with young people **NHSKSF C5:4** Quality – develop a culture that improves quality	**HSC:C2.5** Support inter-disciplinary teams to develop and implement individual programmes of care **H52** Involve customers in the management of the organisation **CBLD:5** Involving children and young people in the management and delivery of service provision
F11 Manage the achievement of customer satisfaction delivering the goal of customer satisfaction with the processes and services being delivered.	**RMA:A2 DANOS:BC2** Manage activities to meet requirements **SA:A22** Manage the use of physical resources **DANOS:BD2** Manage your organisation's facilities **RMRCC:3** Manage a provision which actively promotes children and young people's life chances **RMRCC:5** Manage and engage in work with children and young people, individually and in groups to achieve optimal outcomes **RMA:2 HSC:412** Ensure individuals and groups are supported appropriately when experiencing significant life events **RMRCC:17** Promote and manage a quality provision	**NHSKSF G7:4** Capacity and capability Work in partnership with others to develop and sustain capacity and capability

(Continued)

Functional Area F: Achieving Results (Cont'd)

Generic standards	Specialist standards	Partnership standards
F12 Improve organisational performance – provide the lead for and manage improvements to the services and processes in your area of responsibility; includes sharing knowledge about how improvements can or have been made across the organisation.	**DANOS:BA3** Contribute to the development of organisational performance **DANOS:BA4** Evaluate and improve organisational performance **DANOS:BE1** Establish information management and communication systems **DANOS:BC4** Assure your organisation delivers quality services **RMA:F3** Manage continuous quality improvement **SA:A56** Implement quality assurance systems **NHSKSF: C5:4** Quality – develop a culture that improves quality	**NHSKSF C4:4** Service improvement – work in partnership with others to develop, take forward and evaluate direction, policies and strategies

NHS LQF Setting direction: Drive for results – a strong commitment to making service performance improvements and a determination to achieve positive service outcomes for users **Personal qualities: Drive for improvement** – a deep motivation to improve the performance in the health service **Personal integrity** – a strongly held sense of commitment to openness, honesty, inclusiveness and high standards in undertaking the leadership role

National Standards for Leaders of Children's Centres (DfES 2007)

The Core purposes of Children's centre leaders are that they will make a difference by:

- Establishing and sustaining an environment of challenge and support where children are safe, can flourish and learn.
- Providing the vision, direction and leadership vital to the creation of integrated and comprehensive services for children, mothers, fathers and families.
- Leading the work of the centre to secure its success, its accountability and its continuous improvement. Central to such success is the quality and level of collaboration with other services and the whole of the community.
- Working with and through others to design and shape flexible, responsive services to meet the changing needs of children and families.
- Ensuring that all staff understand children's developmental needs within the context of the family and provide appropriate services that respond to those needs.
- Ensuring that the centre collects and uses all available data to gain a better understanding of the nature and complexity of the local community served by the Children's Centre.
- Using such knowledge and understanding to inform how services are organised and how to offer differentiated services that are responsive to all groups including fathers, children or parents with disabilities or additional needs, and black and minority ethnic communities.

1. Leading Learning and Development	2. Stronger Families, stronger communities	3. Being accountable and responsible
The head of a Children's Centre must be able to show that they can: **1.1** Review and evaluate learning, teaching and care practice to promote improvement in outcomes for children and families with a particular focus on the most disadvantaged. **1.2** Identify, promote and encourage effective practice **1.3** Establish a safe environment in which children can develop and learn **1.4** Develop and foster a learning culture that enables children, families and staff to become successful, enthusiastic and independent learners **1.5** Ensure that staff acknowledge the expertise of parents and find ways to share this knowledge and understanding of individual children's learning at home, in order to work together and improve learning opportunities in the centre **1.6** Help parents overcome barriers such as lack of confidence or poor basic skills and support them to take decisive action to return to study, training and employment **1.7** Respect diversity and respond with sensitivity to different cultures and beliefs and ensure equality of access to learning opportunities **1.8** Regularly review their own practice and take responsibility for their own personal and professional development, seeking support where appropriate **1.9** Create experiences that will inspire children, their families and staff to raise expectations for their own achievement, enjoyment and economic success and make a positive contribution to the community	The head of a Children's Centre must be able to show that they can: **2.1** Raise expectations and aspirations so that families and the local community are encouraged to enjoy new opportunities for learning and better health **2.2** Ensure effective and sustained outreach into the community so that the most disadvantaged families are identified and encouraged to engage with the centre **2.3** Ensure that parents, staff and collaborating agencies use the common assessment framework to identify children's additional needs and share appropriate information about children's health, welfare, learning and development to promote mutual understanding **2.4** Lead a whole centre approach to promoting and publishing the range of activities and opportunities available to parents and the local community (using accessible formats) **2.5** Create imaginative opportunities for ways of including the wider community in the activities of the centre and ensure that parents' views and feedback shape services **2.6** Demonstrate both an awareness of local opportunities such as local regeneration initiatives and the capacity to make best use of their potential resources **2.7** Understand the protocols and procedures to be followed when there are concerns about children's safety and welfare, including the ways that information is shared **2.8** Promote and lead a culture, which reflects and respects the diversity of the local community **2.9** Create and promote positive strategies for challenging all prejudice and dealing with harassment **2.10** Build on the strengths of the child and the family and develop plans and focused interventions that improve outcomes	The head of a Children's Centre must be able to show that they can: **3.1** Accountable to the Management/Governing body, parents, carers, staff, children, the local community and the local authority **3.2** Be responsible for the efficiency, effectiveness and sustainable development of the centre. Central to this is responsibility for the financial management of the centre's current budget and future viability **3.3** Understand, implement and comply with relevant legislation including discrimination legislation, regulations, statutory guidance and inspection requirements. In particular, safeguarding and promoting the welfare of children, and ensuring the welfare of staff and other service users **3.4** Develop, implement, monitor and audit all the Children's Centre's policies, procedures and practices to ensure they comply with legislation, regulations and guidance **3.5** Provide information, advice and support so that the Management/Governing Body can fulfil its responsibilities **3.6** Seek appropriate support to form an objective review of their own performance

4. Shaping the present and creating the future	5. Managing the organisation	6. Building and strengthening teams
The head of a Children's Centre must be able to show that they can: **4.1** Work collaboratively to explore, clarify and develop shared values, principles and vision, recognising the diversity and differences within the centre's local community **4.2** Demonstrate the centre's values, principles and vision in everyday practice **4.3** Be creative, open to innovation, inspire, challenge and empower others to carry the vision forward **4.4** Monitor and evaluate services to ensure that they are relevant, responsive to changing needs and can demonstrate sustained and continuous improvement **4.5** Lead a whole centre approach to continuous organisational self-evaluation **4.6** Demonstrate imaginative ways of working with other local Children's Centres and extended schools to establish collaborative networks that offer mutual benefits and advancement **4.7** Anticipate the need for change and lead its implementation **4.8** Lead a culture of critical reflection and practitioner research, engaging with others to identify, share and promote effective practice that is evidence based **4.9** Work with the governing body/ management committee to develop and implement a strategic plan and accountability systems **4.10** Identify and promote the development of potential future centre leaders	The head of a Children's Centre must be able to show that they can: **5.1** Create organisational structures that support the effective delivery of services, the deployment of staff and good value for money **5.2** Lead the creation, review and implementation of centre development plans and policies that comply with legal requirements **5.3** Ensure that financial management and planning reflect best practice, best value and the centre's aims and priorities **5.4** Sustain and demonstrate personal motivation and be able to motivate all staff **5.5** Prioritise, plan and organise within a complex environment where organizational boundaries are shifting and uncertain **5.6** Devise and refine different models of shared leadership and management **5.7** Ensure that the policies, procedures and practices for safeguarding and promoting the welfare of children are implemented effectively **5.8** Demonstrate a systematic approach to performance management **5.9** Use performance management of staff to set targets, improve practice and raise outcomes	The head of a Children's Centre must be able to show that they can: **6.1** Develop, inspire and motivate multi-disciplinary teams, so that their individual and collective strengths are deployed imaginatively and effectively **6.2** Foster a climate of mutual trust and respect that facilitates effective partnership, communication, collaboration and integrated working practices within and beyond the centre **6.3** Recognise, develop and promote leadership qualities in others, sharing responsibility and authority in imaginative ways **6.4** Maintain, affirm and improve team effectiveness **6.5** Establish effective professional development opportunities to promote successful team working **6.6** Be able to resolve conflict and make difficult or unpopular decisions **6.7** Manage a complex set of relationships with other agencies and encourage constructive and critical debate **6.8** Enable staff to pioneer different ways of working together to improve outcomes for children and families **6.9** Use performance management and professional development systems to set objectives, improve practice and raise outcomes

Teaching standards

The full standards are available at the following web reference http://www.tda.gov.uk/upload/resources/pdf/s/standards_a4.pdf. We have selected the standards that are the most appropriate for this book and are as follows. First from the standards for the end of initial teacher training:

Q5 Recognise and respect the contribution that colleagues, parents and carers can make to the development and well-being of children and young people, and to raising their levels of attainment.

Q6 Have a commitment to collaboration and co-operative working.

Q32 Work as a team member and identify opportunities for working with colleagues, sharing the development of effective practice with them.

Q33 Ensure that colleagues working with them are appropriately involved in supporting learning and understand the roles they are expected to fulfil.

The same standards are required for the end of the induction period and labelled core though there are differences in the numbers assigned, as there is a total increase in the number of standards expected. C 5 and C 6 plus C 40 and 41.

C5 Recognise and respect the contributions that colleagues, parents and carers can make to the development and well-being of children and young people, and to raising their levels of attainment.

C6 Have a commitment to collaboration and co-operative working, where appropriate.

C40 Work as a team member and identify opportunities for working with colleagues, managing their work where appropriate and sharing the development of effective practice with them.

C41 Ensure that colleagues working with them are appropriately involved in supporting learning and understand the roles they are expected to fulfil.

Post threshold the standards are:

P 9 Promote collaboration and work effectively as a team member.

P 10 Contribute to the professional development of colleagues through coaching and mentoring, demonstrating effective practice, and providing advice and feedback.

For the excellent teacher the emphasis on leading others is increased.

E 13 Work closely with leadership teams, taking a leading role in developing, implementing and evaluating policies and practice that contribute to school improvement.

E 14 Contribute to the professional development of colleagues using a broad range of techniques and skills appropriate to their needs so that they demonstrate enhanced and effective practice.

E15 Make well-founded appraisals of situations upon which they are asked to advise, applying high-level skills in classroom observation to evaluate and advise colleagues on their work and devising and implementing effective strategies to meet the learning needs of children and young people leading to improvements in pupil outcomes.

The same is true of the advanced skills teacher with explicit reference to developing leadership throughout the school.

A2 Be part of or work closely with leadership teams, taking a leadership role in developing, implementing and evaluating policies and practice in their own and other workplaces that contribute to school improvement.

A3 Possess the analytical, interpersonal and organisational skills necessary to work effectively with staff and leadership teams beyond their own school.

The Standards are set out in six key non-hierarchical areas. These six key areas, when taken together, represent the role of the head teacher.

- Shaping the Future
- Leading Learning and Teaching
- Developing Self and Working with Others
- Managing the Organisation
- Securing Accountability
- Strengthening Community

Shaping the future

Knowledge

Local, national and global trends

Ways to build communicate and implement a shared vision

Strategic planning processes

Strategies for communication both within and beyond the school

New technologies, their use and impact

Leading change, creativity and innovation

Professional Qualities

Is committed to:

A collaborative school vision of excellence and equity that sets high standards for every pupil

The setting and achieving of ambitious, challenging goals and targets

The use of appropriate new technologies

Inclusion and the ability and right of all to be the best they can be

Is able to:

Think strategically, build and communicate a coherent vision in a range of compelling ways

Inspire, challenge, motivate and empower others to carry the vision forward

Model the values and vision of the school

Actions

Ensures the vision for the school is clearly articulated, shared, understood and acted upon effectively by all

Works within the school community to translate the vision into agreed objectives and operational plans which will promote and sustain school improvement

Demonstrates the vision and values in everyday work and practice

Motivates and works with others to create a shared culture and positive climate

Ensures creativity, innovation and the use of appropriate new technologies to achieve excellence

Ensures that strategic planning takes account of the diversity, values and experience of the school and community at large

Leading learning and teaching

Knowledge

Knows about:

Strategies for raising achievement and achieving excellence

The development of a personalised learning culture within the school

Models of learning and teaching

The use of new and emerging technologies to support learning and teaching

Principles of effective teaching and assessment for learning

Models of behaviour and attendance management

Strategies for ensuring inclusion, diversity and access

Curriculum design and management

Tools for data collection and analysis

Using research evidence to inform teaching and learning

Monitoring and evaluating performance

School self-evaluation

Strategies for developing effective teachers

Professional Qualities

Is committed to:

The raising of standards for all in the pursuit of excellence

The continuing learning of all members of the school community

The entitlement of all pupils to effective teaching and learning

Choice and flexibility in learning to meet the personalised learning needs of every child

Is able to:

Demonstrate personal enthusiasm for and commitment to the learning process

Demonstrate the principles and practice of effective teaching and learning

Access, analyse and interpret information

Initiate and support research and debate about effective learning and teaching and develop relevant strategies for performance improvement

Acknowledge excellence and challenge poor performance across the school

Developing self and working with others

Knowledge

Knows about:

The significance of interpersonal relationships, adult learning and models of continuing professional development (CPD)

Strategies to promote individual and team development

Building and sustaining a learning community

The relationship between managing performance, CPD and sustained school improvement

The impact of change on organisations and individuals

Professional Qualities

Is committed to:

Effective working relationships

Shared leadership

Effective team working

Continuing professional development for self and all others within the school

Is able to:

Foster an open, fair, equitable culture and manage conflict

Develop, empower and sustain individuals and teams

Collaborate and network with others within and beyond the school

Challenge, influence and motivate others to attain high goals

Give and receive effective feedback and act to improve personal performance

Accept support from others including colleagues, governors and the LA

Managing the organisation

Knowledge

Knows about:

Models of organisations and principles of organisational development

Principles and models of self-evaluation

Principles and practice of earned autonomy

Principles and strategies of school improvement

Project management for planning and implementing change

Policy creation, through consultation and review

Informed decision-making

Strategic financial planning, budgetary management and principles of best value

Performance management

Personnel, governance, security and access issues relating to the diverse use of school facilities

Legal issues relating to managing a school including Equal Opportunities, Race Relations, Disability, Human Rights and Employment legislation

The use of new and emerging technologies to enhance organisational effectiveness

Professional Qualities

Is committed to:

Distributed leadership and management

The equitable management of staff and resources

The sustaining of personal motivation and that of all staff

The developing and sustaining of a safe, secure and healthy school environment

Collaborating with others in order to strengthen the school's organizational capacity and contribute to the development of capacity in other schools

Is able to:

Establish and sustain appropriate structures and systems

Manage the school efficiently and effectively on a day-to-day basis

Delegate management tasks and monitor their implementation

Prioritise, plan and organise themselves and others

Make professional, managerial and organisational decisions based on informed judgements

Think creatively to anticipate and solve problems

Securing accountability

Knowledge

Knows about:

Statutory educational frameworks, including governance

Public services policy and accountability frameworks, including self-evaluation and multi-agency working

The contribution that education makes to developing, promoting and sustaining a fair and equitable society

The use of a range of evidence, including performance data, to support, monitor, evaluate and improve aspects of school life, including challenging poor performance

The principles and practice of quality assurance systems, including school review, self-evaluation and performance management

Stakeholder and community engagement in, and accountability for, the success and celebration of the school's performance

Professional Qualities

Is committed to:

Principles and practice of school self-evaluation

The school working effectively and efficiently towards the academic, spiritual, moral, social, emotional and cultural development of all its pupils

Individual, team and whole-school accountability for pupil learning outcomes

Is able to:

Demonstrate political insight and anticipate trends

Engage the school community in the systematic and rigorous self-evaluation of the work of the school

Collect and use a rich set of data to understand the strengths and weaknesses of the school

Combine the outcomes of regular school self-review with external evaluations in order to develop the school

Actions

Fulfils commitments arising from contractual accountability to the governing body

Develops a school ethos, which enables everyone to work collaboratively, share knowledge and understanding, celebrate success and accept responsibility for outcomes

Ensures individual staff accountabilities are clearly defined, understood and agreed and are subject to rigorous review and evaluation

Works with the governing body (providing information, objective advice and support) to enable it to meet its responsibilities

Develops and presents a coherent, understandable and accurate account of the school's performance to a range of audiences including governors, parents and carers

Reflects on personal contribution to school achievements and takes account of feedback from others

Strengthening community

Knowledge

Knows about:

Current issues and future trends that impact on the school community

The rich and diverse resources within local communities – both human and physical

The wider curriculum beyond school and the opportunities it provides for pupils and the school community

Models of school, home, community and business partnerships

The work of other agencies and opportunities for collaboration

Strategies, which encourage parents and carers to support their children's learning

The strengths, capabilities and objectives of other schools

Professional Qualities

Is committed to:

Effective teamwork within the school and with external partners

Work with other agencies for the well being of all pupils and their families

Involvement of parents and the community in supporting the learning of children and in defining and realising the school vision

Collaboration and networking with other schools to improve outcomes

Is able to:

Recognise and take account of the richness and diversity of the school's communities

Engage in a dialogue, which builds partnerships and community consensus on values, beliefs and shared responsibilities

Listen to, reflect and act on community feedback

Build and maintain effective relationships with parents, carers, partners and the community, that enhance the education of all pupils.

References

Academy for Sustainable Communities (ASC) (2006) *Leadership of Place.* Leeds

Alimo-Metcalf, B. and Alban Metcalf, J. (2003) Leadership in Public Sector Organizations, In Storey (ed.) *Leadership Organisations: Current Issues and Key Trends.* London: Routledge

Armstrong, D. J. and Cole, P. (2002) Managing Distances and Differences in Geographically Distributed Work Groups. In P. Hinds and S. Kiesler (eds), *Distributed Work* (pp.167–186). Massachusetts Institute of Technology

Atwater, L. E. and Yammarino, F. J. (1992) Does self-other agreement on leadership perceptions moderate the validity of leadership and performance predictions? *Personnel Psychology*, 45, 141–164.

Aubrey, C. (2007) *Leading and Managing in the Early Years.* London: Sage

Audit Commission www.audit-commission.gov.uk (accessed 21.05.08)

Bass, B. (1989) *Stogdill's Handbook of Leadership: A Survey of Theory and Research.* New York: Free Press

— (1990) From transactional to transformational leadership: learning to share the vision. Organizational Dynamics, Vol. 18, Issue 3, Winter, 1990, 19–31.

Bass, B. and Avolio, B. (1993) Transformational leadership and organizational culture. Public Administration Quarterly, 17, 112–121

Bennis, W. and Nanus B. (1985) Leaders. New York: Harper and Row

Bergquist, W., Betwee, J. and Meuel, D. (1995) Building Strategic Relationships : How To Extend Your Organization's Reach Through Partnerships Alliances and Joint Ventures. San Francisco: Jossey-Bass Publishers

Blair, G.M. (1991) Basic Management: The Essential Skills. Chartwell Bratt Ltd: IEE Management Journal

Blake, R. R. and Mouton, J. S. (1985) The Managerial Grid III: The Key to Leadership Excellence. Houston: Gulf Publishing Co

Bolman, L. and Deal, T. (1991) Reframing Organisations. San Francisco: Jossey-Bass

Burns, James MacGregor. (1978) Leadership. New York:Harper & Row, Publishers, Inc

Burns, R. (1786) To a Louse on Seeing One on a Lady's Bonnet, at Church http://www.nls.uk/burns/mainsite/killl/kill.htm (National library of Scotland's reference for the original manuscript, accessed 11.11.08)

Clutterbuck, D. and Megginson, D., (1999) Mentoring Executives and Directors. Oxford: Butterworth-Heinemann

Conger, J. A. (1989) The Charismatic Leader. San Francisco: Jossey-Bass

Covey, S. (1992) The Seven Habits of Highly Effective People: Powerful Lessons in Personal Change. London: Simon & Schuster Ltd

CWDC (2007) Guidance to the Standards for the Award of Early years Professional Status. Leeds :CWDC

DfES/DWP (2003) *National standards for under 8s day care and childminding* http://www.surestart.gov.uk/_doc/P0000411.PDF (accessed 31.09.08) Nottingham: DfES

DfES (2004a) Every Child Matters: Change for Children. Nottingham: DfES

— (2004b) National Standards for Headteachers. Nottingham: DfES

— (2007) National Standards for Leaders of Children's Centres. Nottingham: DfES Publications

DiMaggio, P. J. and Powell, W. W. (1983) The iron cage revisited: institutional isomorphism and collective rationality in organizational fields. American Sociological Review, 48(2), 147–160

Doz, Y. L. and Hamel, G. (1998) Alliance Advantage : The Art of Creating Value through Partnering. Harvard: Harvard Business School Press, p. xv

Easterby-Smith, M., Burgoyne, J. and Araujo, L. (eds) (1999) Organizational Learning and the Learning Organization, London: Sage

Ebbeck, M. and Waniganayake, M. (2003) Early Childhood Professionals. Leading Today and Tomorrow. Eastgardens, NSW: MacLennan and Petty Pty Ltd.

Fiedler, F. E. (1964) A contingency model of leadership effectiveness. In L. Berkowitz (ed.), Advances in Experimental Social Psychology, New York: Academic Press

Frost, N. (2005) Professionalism, Partnership and Joined-up Thinking: A Research Review of Frontline Working with Children and Families. Totnes Devon: Blacklers

Goffman, E. (1959) The Presentation of Self in Everyday Life. Garden City, New York: Doubleday

Goleman, D., Boyatzis, R. and McKee, A. (2004) Primal Leadership. Harvard: HBS Press

Grant, D. and Oswick, C. (eds) (1996) Metaphor and Organizations. Thousand Oaks, California: Sage Publications

Gronn, P. (2002) Distributed Leadership. In K. Leithwood, P. Hallinger, K. Seashore-Louis, G. Furman-Brown, P. Gronn, W. Mulford and K. Riley (eds), Second International Handbook of Educational Leadership and Administration. Dordrecht: Kluwer

Harvey, J. and Katz, C. (1985) If I'm So Successful, Why Do I Feel Like a Fake? The Imposter Phenomenon. New York: St. Martin's.

Hickman, C. (1990) Mind of a Manager, Soul of a Leader. New York: John Wiley & Sons

Hirsh, W. (2000) Succession Planning Demystified. Brighton: Institute for Employment Studies.

House, R. J. (1976) A 1976 Theory of Charismatic Leadership. Working Paper Series 76–06

Hunt, J. G. (1991) Leadership: A new Synthesis. London: Sage

Jaques, E. and Clement, S. D. (1994) Executive Leadership: A Practical Guide to Managing Complexity. Cambridge, MA: Carson-Hall & Co. Publishers

Kelley, R. (1992) The Power of Followership. New York: Bantam Dell

Kets de Vries, Manfred. F. R. (2005) 'The Dangers of Feeling like a Fake', Harvard Business Review, 1–9

Kotter, J. (1996) Leading Change. Harvard: Harvard Business School Press

Kouzes, J. M. and Posner, B. Z. (1987) The Leadership Challenge. San Francisco: Jossey-Bass

Lakoff, G. and Johnson, M. (1999) Metaphors We Live By (2 nd ed.). Chicago: University of Chicago Press

Leadership Centre for Local Government (2006) The Politics of Place. London: Leading Edge Publications

Local Government Act 2000. Crown Copyright http://www.opsi.gov.uk/Acts/acts2000/ukpga_20000022_en_1 (accessed 21.09.08)

Luft, J. and Ingham, H. (1955) 'The Johari window, a graphic model of interpersonal awareness', Proceedings of the western training laboratory in group development. Los Angeles: UCLA

Morgan, (1986) Images of Organization. London: Sage

McDonnell, F. and Zutshi, H. (2006) (HZ Management and Training Consultancy) Mapping of Leadership and Management Standards for Social Care Leeds: Skills for Care

McGregor, D. (1960) The Human Side of Enterprise. New York: McGraw-Hill

Muijs D., Aubrey C., Harris A., Briggs M. (2004) 'How do they manage?', Journal Of Early Childhood Research, 12 (2), 157–169 (1476–718 X)

National Association of Social Workers (1999) *Code of Ethics.* www.socialworkers.org/pubs/code/code.asp (accessed 21.09.08)

Nickelback (2000) 'Leader of Men' from the album *The State*

Nelson, B. (1997) *1001 Ways to Reward Employees.* New York: Workman Publishing Company

J. Nelson, J. and S. Zadek (2000) *Partnership Alchemy: New Social Partnerships in Europe.* Copenhagen: The Copenhagen Centre

Parsloe, E. (1999) *The Manager as Coach and Mentor.* London: CIPD

Parker Follett, M. (1918) *The New State-Group Organization, the Solution for Popular Government.* New York: Longman, Green and Co

Piaget, J. (1977) The Development of Thought: Equilibration of Cognitive Structure. New York: Viking

Pearn, M. and Kandola, P. (1993) *Job Analysis: A Manager's Guide,* 2nd ed.

London: Institute of Personnel Management

Richardson, C. (1996) Snakes and ladders? The differing career patterns of male and female accountants, *Women in Management Review,* Vol. 11 No.4, pp. 13–19

Ringer, T. M. (2002) *Group Action.* Philadelphia: Jessica Kingsley Publishers

Rodd, J. (1996) Towards a toplogy of leadership for the early childhood professional of the 21st century, *Early Childhood Development and Care,* 120: 119–26

— (1997) Learning to be leaders: perceptions of early childhood professional about leadership roles and responsibilities. *Early Years,* 18(1): 40–46

— (1999) *Leadership in Early Childhood.* Buckingham: Open University Press

— (2006) *Leadership in Early Childhood: The Pathway to Professionalism.* Maidenhead: Open University Press

Rosener, J. B. (1995) *American's Competitive Secret: Utilizing Women as A Management Strategy.* New York: Oxford University Press

Sagawa, S. and Segal, E. (2000) Common Interest Common Good : Creating Value Through Business and Social Sector Partnerships. Harvard: Harvard Business School Press

Schein, E. (1996) *Career Anchors – discovering your real values* – Oxford: Pfeiffer,

Schön, D. A. (1983) The *Reflective Practitioner.* New York: Basic Books

Scrivens, C. 'Professional leadership in early childhood: The New Zealand kindergarten experience' www.aare.edu.au/99pap/scr99178.htm (accessed 2008)

Shamir, B. (1995) 'Social distance and charisma: theoretical notes and an exploratory study'. *The Leadership Quarterly,* 19–47

Simon, H. (1991) Bounded Rationality and Organizational Learning. *Organization Science* 2(1): 125–134

Stacey, R. D. (1996) *Complexity and Creativity in Organizations.* San Francisco: Berrett-Koehler Publishers

Stogdill, R. (1974) *Handbook of Leadership: A Survey of Theory and Research.* New York: Simon & Schuster Adult Publishing Group

Surestart http://www.surestart.gov.uk/surestartservices/settings/surestartchildrenscentres/ (accessed 2008)

Tuckman, B. (1965) Developmental sequence in small groups. *Psychological bulletin,* 63, 384–399

Watson Wyatt (2008) *Poor Leadership in Motivating Poorer-Performing Staff* (accessed 21.09.08)

Wenger, E. (1998) *Communities of Practice: Learning, Meaning, and Identity.* Cambridge: Cambridge University Press

West, M. et al. (2001–2008) Aston papers http://www.abs.aston.ac.uk/newweb/research/publications/default.asp?fldpublicationtype=WORKING%20PAPER&fldPublicationyear=2001 (accessed 21.09.08)

White, J. B. and Prywes, Y. (2007) *The Nature of Leadership: Reptiles, Mammals, and the Challenge of Becoming a Great Leader.* AMACOM Div American Management Association. New York: AMACOM

Winslow-Taylor, F. (1911 original publication date) (1997 paperback) *The Principles of Scientific Management.* Mineola, NY: Dover Publications

WLN (Women's Leadership Network) (March 2007) London: Women's Leadership Network/Leadership for Learning and Skills Sector

Index